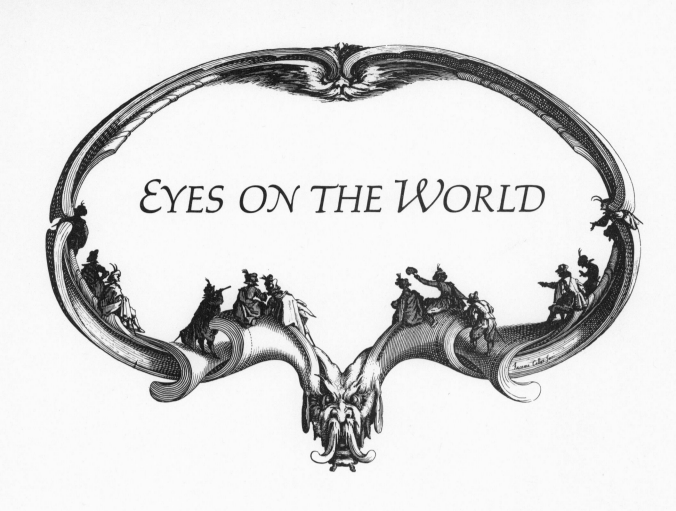

EYES ON THE WORLD

EYES ON THE

The Story & Work

His Gypsies, Beggars,
War'' and Other Famous
Together with an

by ESTHER AVERILL

WORLD
of Jacques Callot

Festivals, "Miseries of
Etchings and Engravings,
Account of his Days

Funk & Wagnalls, New York

For kind assistance in connection with this book, the author wishes to express her gratitude to the following institutions and individuals: Cooper Union whose Museum for the Arts of Decoration, under Christian Rohlfing, Administrator, offered the facilities of the Print Room and the Library; the Frick Art Reference Library which, under Mrs. Henry W. Howell, Jr., Librarian, made available the resouces of the Reference Room and the extensive collection of photographs (special thanks to Hope Mathewson and Mildred Steinbach); The Metropolitan Museum of Art where the Print Department, under A. Hyatt Mayor, Curator, opened its very rich collection of Callot etchings and engravings (special thanks to Janet S. Byrne of the Print Room); and The New York Public Library where members of the Prints Division, under Karl Kup, Curator, not only helped the author with Callot but encouraged her work. It was here that she began her research, and in this Print Room Elizabeth Roth patiently guided her toward the print world of the experts.

Text copyright © 1969 by Esther Averill
Map copyright © 1969 by Laszlo Matulay
First published in the United States of America, 1969,
by Funk & Wagnalls, *A Division of* Reader's Digest Books, Inc.
Designed by Wells-Jeffers
Library of Congress Catalogue Card Number: 68-13077
Printed in the United States of America
1

Picture credits: Bibliothèque Nationale, 46; The Cooper Union Museum, 105 [top]; Musée du Louvre (Cabinet des Dessins) 29, 53 [top]; The Metropolitan Museum of Art, 56 [right], 57 [right], 80, 81, (Bequest of Edwin De T. Bechtel) 34-5, 36, 54, 57 [left], 68-9, 76-7, 94 [bottom left], 96-7, 100-1, 102, 103, 105 [bottom], 160, (Gift of Theodore de Witt) 132-3, (Dick Fund) 4, 22-3, 56 [left], 94 [top left], 125, 126, (Bequest of Albert Ten Eyck Gardner) 31, (Rogers Fund) 10-11, 12-13, 18, 91, 149 [bottom], (Gift of Paul J. Sachs) 53 [bottom], (Gift of Henry Walters) 156-7, (Whittelsey Fund) 74-75; National Gallery of Art (R. L. Baumfeld Collection) 84-5, (L. J. Rosenwald Collection) 92, 93, 94 [top right], 94 [bottom right], 114-5, 116, 117, 118, 128-9, 130, 136-7; The New York Public Library (Prints Division) 8, 17, 19, 20-1, 38, 39, 40, 41, 42-3, 44, 48-9, 55, 60, 62-3, 71, 72, 110, 111, 138, 142 [top], 142-3, 149 [top], 151.

To Louise Seaman Bechtel,
Generous with her Knowledge of Callot
and her Understanding of Books for young People

Contents

Illustrations

(Dimensions are based on those given
in Jacques Callot by J. Lieure)

ETCHINGS, ENGRAVINGS,
AND DRAWINGS BY JACQUES CALLOT

	Plate number	Title	Size of original work (height x width, in inches)
City Scenes	24	Ponte Vecchio	2¼ x 3¼
	34	Public Square at Nancy	6¹¹⁄₁₆ x 20¼
	63	View of the Louvre	6¹¹⁄₁₆ x 13⅜
Drawings	10	Seated Man	3¾ x 2⅜
	17	The Slave Market	4⅝ x 8¾
Festivals and Celebrations	14	The War of Love (general view)	8¹⁵⁄₁₆ x 11¹⁵⁄₁₆
	15	First Intermezzo	11⅜ x 8³⁄₁₆
	21	Flag Play on the Piazza Santa Croce	2⅛ x 3⅛
	23	Fireworks on the River Arno	2¹⁄₁₆ x 3³⁄₁₆
	32	The Fan	8¹⁵⁄₁₆ x 11¹⁵⁄₁₆
	33	Impruneta Fair	17¼ x 26¹³⁄₁₆
	48	Combat at the Barrier	6 x 9⁹⁄₁₆
	49	Entry of Three Nobles	5¹³⁄₁₆ x 8¹¹⁄₁₆
	50	Entry of Two Nobles on a Dragon	6 x 9⁹⁄₁₆
	51	Entry of Duke Charles IV	6 x 9⁹⁄₁₆
Landscapes	25	On the River	4⁹⁄₁₆ x 9⅞
	26	The Water Mill	4⅝ x 9¹⁵⁄₁₆
	27	Deer Hunt near the Manor	4⅝ x 9⅞
	28	The Small Port	3⁵⁄₁₆ x 8¹¹⁄₁₆
Military History	55	Siege of Breda (complete work)	48⁹⁄₁₆ x 55½
	56	Siege of Breda (lower right plate)	25¹⁵⁄₁₆ x 18⁹⁄₁₆
	57	Siege of Breda (lower center plate)	25³⁄₁₆ x 19¾
	58	Siege of Breda (lower left plate)	26 x 18⁵⁄₁₆

ETCHINGS AND ENGRAVINGS BY OTHER 17th-CENTURY ARTISTS

Introduction

Detail, plate 21

Jacques Callot was the first great reporter-artist of the Western world. His field was 17th-century Europe, and through his hundreds of prints he recorded vital moments in the history of Italy, the Spanish Netherlands, France, and his native Lorraine.

Monarchs, noblemen, friars, and booksellers commissioned him to etch or engrave many of the copper plates from which the prints were made. The commissioned work included portraits, festival books, religious keepsakes and emblems, and pictures of funerals and sieges. For his own satisfaction, Callot etched beggars, gypsies, actors, and other striking characters who were part of the contemporary scene. Callot also produced "fantasies," which were either lovely or terrifying. His prints were bought by rich and poor, and treasured by collectors. His story can be read, without words, in the great Lieure picture-catalog which shows more than 1,400 of his prints. The man from Lorraine is best known in France, where people call him "the father of French etching."

During World War II, Callot's native city of Nancy became a supply center for American troops, who captured it as they fought their way from France into Germany. It was a key crossroads, as it had been in Callot's day. Our soldiers passed his statue. Many of them sent home post cards of his celebrated "Miseries of War." Those little

1

views, to them, seemed quaint, though probably symbolic of many scenes which they saw in their own war.

Soon after World War II, Nancy's old ducal palace, now a fine museum, was reopened. There, today, besides Callot's prints and plates, a visitor can see many relics from the period of that city's most famous son.

In the United States, the prints of Callot have long ranked high in the minds of eminent collectors. In recent years, several fine, extensive collections of these works have been generously donated, for the enjoyment of the public, to museums and other institutions. Such institutions have staged local exhibitions of Callot's work and have helped to send at least two important shows on tour across the country. Callot prints loaned by the Metropolitan Museum of Art went on the road under the auspices of the American Federation of Arts in a show called "Two French Realists: Daumier and Callot" and were seen at art centers, including schools and universities, throughout the nation from October, 1959, through October, 1961. The Smithsonian Institution, in 1964 and 1965, circulated nearly all his work in a traveling exhibition, "Prints by Jacques Callot," compiled from collections in the National Gallery.

Callot stands as a milestone in the history of printmaking. During his lifetime, the European art of engraving in order to reproduce pictures on paper was not much more than a couple of centuries old. Most of Callot's great predecessors engraved on wood blocks. From the late 1400's on, some worked on metal. They, or their apprentices, inked the engraved wood blocks or metal plates and printed them with a handpress. Most prints were made on such excellent handmade paper that they had a good chance of surviving up to the present time.

Before engraving was introduced into Europe, people sought their pictures of the world in the paintings, sculpture, and stained-glass windows of churches, in tapestries, in rare, hand-illustrated books, or in other individual works of art, all made by hand. These single objects might be copied by hand, but they could never be precisely duplicated nor, because of the labor involved, could many copies be executed. Prints, consequently, were a boon. Yet, in spite of their popularity, no organized attempt was made to issue them as up-to-the-minute reports on what was happening in the world. The process of engraving required too much slow toil by hand. Besides, all forms of communication were slow. No daily newspapers existed, and nothing moved overland faster than a horse.

Jacques Callot, born at the dawn of a new age, possessed a lively spirit, a roving eye, and an endless curiosity about the world through which he moved. He liked to work on copper plates, and since his impulse was to record what attracted him, he adopted and perfected the speedy form of engraving known as "etching." Thus he became the timely reporter of life as he experienced it while traveling the highways and byways of Western Europe.

The kind of art for which Callot has so long been famous, that of etching and engraving, has been pursued further through the years. Print departments are now found in most large museums and in some colleges and libraries. When they offer exhibits of the history of printmaking, there will always be one or more prints by Callot. In this book, therefore, several detailed descriptions of this art medium, as practiced by Callot, have been included. They may lead you to look at all such art, old or new, with a greater understanding and to see the progress and changes in Callot's style with a keener eye. I hope you will find him a stimulating friend to keep in your mind, one who has illuminated both the art history and the human history of a vivid but troubled era in 17th-century Europe.

E.A.

New York City
March, 1968

IACOBVS CALLOT
CALCOGRAPHVS AQVA FORTI NANCEII IN LOTHARINGIA. NOBILIS.

Ant. van Dyck pinxit.
Lorsterman sculp.

Cum priuilegio

ONE

Boyhood at Nancy

Plate 1. Portrait of
Jacques Callot. Engraved by
Lucas Vosterman in 1627,
this print shows a youthful
but serious Callot at
work on a drawing.
He wears the medal
and gold chain given him
by Florentine Grand Duke
Cosimo de' Medici.
The inscription, written in
Latin, identifies Jacques
Callot as an etcher and
a nobleman of Lorraine.
Vosterman based his engraving
on an earlier painting
done by Anthony Van Dyck

According to legend, the first sounds Jacques Callot heard when he was born in 1592 were those of a battle at the walls of Nancy. His native city was the capital of Lorraine, a small European duchy whose ruler was waging war with King Henry IV of France.

Lorraine was a land of fertile, rolling farms, abundant crops, and fat cattle. Its hills were mined for silver, iron, and copper, and many people in the Lorraine of Callot's day were adept at metalwork. The duchy was famous for her bellfounders and for her goldsmiths who skillfully engraved coins, medals, and suits of armor.

For Jacques Callot, the events, character, and people of Lorraine were to have great meaning. That tiny land of 12,000 square miles, lying between France, Germany, and the Netherlands, made important early impressions on the sensitive perception of the Western world's first great reporter-artist.

When Jacques was born his father, Jean Callot, was serving as an archer in the bodyguard of the ruling Duke Charles III of Lorraine. Charles is known in Lorraine history as "Charles the Great" because he was one of the better sovereigns of the realm. Historians do not blame him for the strange and terrible witch burnings that seared his duchy; these "punishments" also took place elsewhere in Europe. Charles's worst error was the futile claim he laid to the throne of France. But the battles fought in Lorraine on that account ended when Jacques was about two years old.

Charles III then settled down to encourage industry, the arts, and learning in his duchy. He had already done much in those areas by importing craftsmen and artists from abroad and by establishing a fine university at Pont-à-Mousson. In his capital city of Nancy he had started to build a whole new section, the "New Town," because the section known as the "Old Town," with nearly 7,000 inhabitants, had outgrown its medieval confines. Now that peace had come, the building of the New Town went more rapidly, and life all over Nancy held enchantments for a small boy with roving eyes.

There was plenty for Jacques to see in the Old Town where he lived with his parents, his older brother, and younger brothers and sisters. Nancy was a crossroads city, and Jacques' own street was a thoroughfare for travelers. There they often paused to eat or sleep at one of the inns, perhaps at the Tavern of the Three Kings, which had once belonged to Jacques' grandfather, Claude Callot. Afterward they would resume their journeys on horseback, by coach, or on foot, heading north to the Netherlands, east to Germany, west to France, or south, all the way beyond the Alps, to Italy.

Jacques' street offered him other delights, for within the gray, weathered, stone houses that were huddled together shoulder-to-shoulder there lived persons who worked for the splendor of Duke Charles III and his court. There was the saddlemaker who manipulated the tangy-smelling leather so that the Duke and his followers might go hunting in comfort and style. Nearby was the tailor who cut and turned colored satins and velvets into fine gowns for the ladies. Painters devised pictures to ornament the interior of the ducal palace, which stood just around the corner on a street of its own.

Straight up from the Old Town rose the handsome, long,

Detail, plate 34.
These tall, gabled buildings in the city of Nancy stood next to one wing of the ducal palace. The numerous figures and tiny details, such as the horse-drawn carriages, are typical of Callot's work

three-storied façade of the palace, flanked at one end by the Chapel of St. George and at the other by the Church of the Franciscans. In the church the previous dukes of Lorraine lay buried, and in its cloisters reposed the body of grandfather Claude Callot. The main entrance to the palace was ornamented with pillars and carvings, and above it could be seen the statue of old Duke Antoine on his stone horse. The vibrant life inside the palace nourished Jacques' taste for worldly elegance and prepared him for moving at ease through other courts of Western Europe.

⁂ LIFE IN THE DUCAL PALACE

Jacques knew much about life in the ducal palace of Nancy long before he saw it with his own eyes. Not only was his father an archer in the ducal bodyguard, but, in addition, the Callots belonged to the nobility, and hence enjoyed relations with the court. Jacques could thank his grandfather for the family's noble rank. Claude had prospered as the tavernkeeper of The Three Kings, and then, after rendering services to Charles III, he had been ennobled. Consequently, Jacques' father was a nobleman, and so was Jacques. As proof of nobility the Callots possessed a family badge, or coat of arms, displaying five gold stars on an azure field [PL. 2]. Above the shield was an arm brandishing a battle-axe.

Jacques' mother, in her own right, also belonged to the world of ducal courts. She was Renée Brunehault, daughter of a doctor to the previous Duchess of Lorraine, Christine of Denmark. Thus the boy learned from his father and mother what life was like at the court of Charles III.

The ducal palace contained a maze of rooms, apartments, and vaulted halls thronging with relatives, guests, and servants, among whom the aging, widowed Charles III lived and kept his court with the traditional magnificence of the dukes of Lorraine. The magnificence was interwoven with social graces borrowed from the court of France. Charles, like his immediate predecessors, had been educated in France, not because French was the principal language spoken in his duchy, but rather because the House of Lorraine enjoyed close family connections with the big monarchy across the border. These ties had been strengthened by Charles's youthful marriage to a French king's daughter, Claude of France. Thus at the Nancy court the silks, satins, and velvets worn by the lords and ladies showed the influence of Paris styles, while manners, music, dancing, and plays also reflected French taste.

Court life was brought still closer to Jacques when he was eight years old. His father then received the court post of Pursuivant of Arms, a low-ranking office in heraldry. The appointment came as a reward for duties described in a ducal statement as "good and pleasing services which he [Jean Callot] has rendered us in the recent wars and previously and such as he is still rendering at the present time, as much in his capacity of archer in our bodyguard as in other missions and special assignments for which we have employed him. . . ."

One function of the courtly institution known as heraldry was to issue and control the use of coats of arms. This made necessary the painting of heraldic emblems for documentary purposes and, fortunately, Jean Callot could paint coats of arms. He made no claim to being a skilled professional artist, but a gentlemanly talent with the brush enabled him to be a herald painter. He painted, or supervised the painting of, coats of arms for the House of Lorraine and for allied houses whenever such emblems were needed to decorate banners, trumpets, candles, and other paraphernalia used in court ceremonials and festivities. His talent helped him finally to achieve the highest heraldic post in Lorraine, Herald of Arms. In his new capacity he assumed charge of ducal ceremonials. Thus he became Master of the Ceremonies at one of Europe's most brilliant small

Plate 2. Callot Coat of Arms. Etched by the artist in his later years, this symbol of nobility was awarded to his grandfather, Claude, who had been a tavernkeeper

courts. A love of court pageantry was to shine in the etchings and engravings created by his son in a later day.

YOUNG CALLOT WISHES TO BECOME AN ARTIST

Jean Callot sent young Jacques to the local school, hoping the boy would acquire enough education to be either the family's next Herald of Arms or the priest of a benefice, or endowed parish, controlled by the Callots in the neighboring village of Bainville-sur-Madon. Sieur Jean opposed Jacques' desire to become a full-time artist.

Jacques, however, cared little for his schoolwork. His old biographer, the French art historian Felibien, wrote that "From his earliest youth Jacques revealed his love of drawing. For at school he filled his books with various pictures, and all the while his parents were making him study, he found no greater pleasure than planning the moments when he might relax and amuse himself."

In the streets of Nancy the boy found many scenes to attract his eyes and inspire drawings. He might see a robber dangling from the gallows or a witch burning at the stake. But he preferred the wandering acrobats and the players who performed in the open. He loved carnival time, when the Church encouraged dancing and merrymaking before the fasts of Lent and when the Duke offered tournaments in the public square. Jacques saw an endless pageant of life to which the wide world, not just the court of Nancy, contributed. No wonder he was bored with the art of heraldry; those handsome coats of arms were too motionless for his lively temperament. He knew that when he grew up he wished to be a full-time, professional artist like those excellent painters, Bellange and Henriet, and those sculptors and engravers of coins and seals employed by Duke Charles to adorn his palace or commemorate notable events. The boy craved more time with art.

✳ THE BOY RUNS AWAY FROM HOME

Felibien tells us that Jacques, when he was barely 12 years old, ran off to Italy, the land of every artist's dream, and that the boy made the long journey southward to the Italian city of Florence (more than 400 miles) with a band of gypsies [PL. 3, 4]. Felibien's story is so famous that it should be read as it first appeared:

> At last, having heard of the beautiful things to be seen in Italy, he [Jacques] was seized with such a violent desire to go there that, even though he was only 11 or 12 years old, he resolved to leave his father's house, and without providing for a means of subsisting during his journey, he departed secretly and took the road to Rome.

The little money he had was soon spent, so that, finding himself in need, he joined a band of Gypsies who were also going to Italy, and without thinking of the company to which he was entrusting himself, or the hardships of the trip or the shameful life he was leading, he went with them to Florence. There he separated from them.

An officer of the Grand Duke having seen him by chance, asked him from where he came and what he was doing, and as he had a pleasant countenance, he took charge of him and sent him to sketch in the studio of a painter named Canta-Gallina, who had a good reputation and specialized in engraving. He learned something during the short time he was with his master, for having always had a great desire to see Rome [which was 150 miles south of Florence], he begged so hard that the master permitted him to go there and assisted him with money for the journey.

Plate 3. Gypsies on the Road: The Advance Guard. Callot etched this glimpse of gypsy life long after his work had become famous. As a boy he traveled with gypsies southeast to the city of Florence

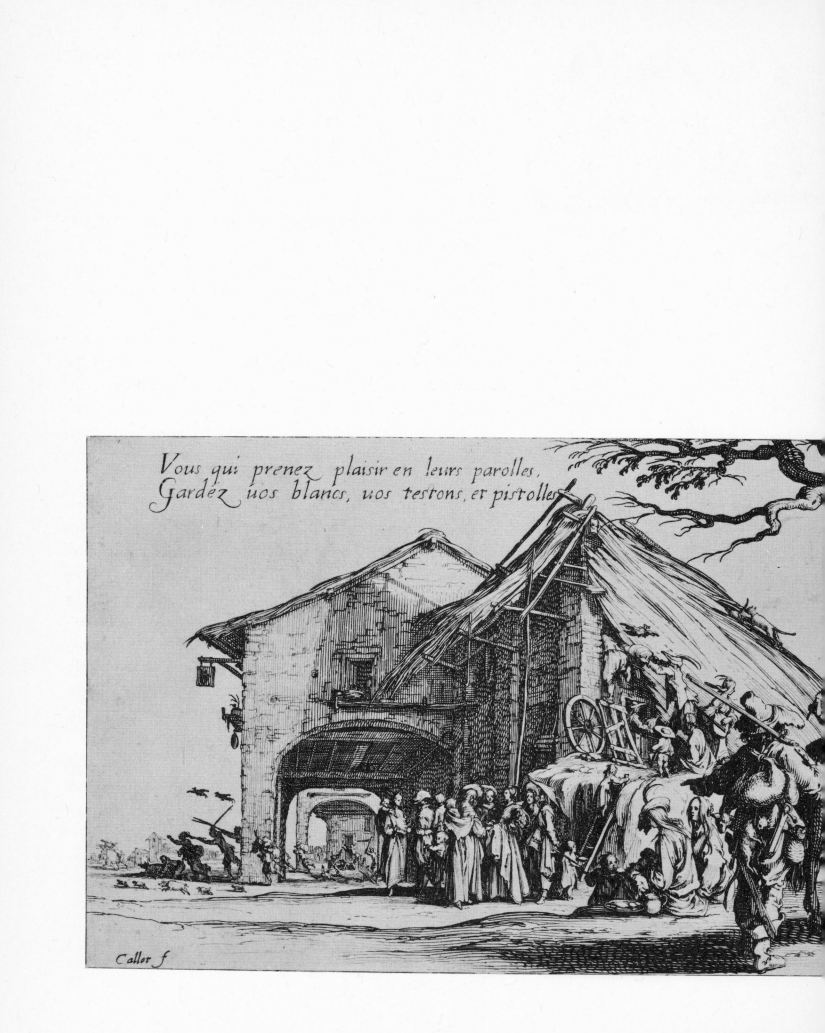

Vous qui prenez plaisir en leurs parolles,
Gardez uos blancs, uos testons, et pistolles

Callot f

Detail, plate 4

Plate 4. The Fortune Tellers. Here Callot shows gypsies pausing to relax and tell fortunes. The inscription warns viewers: "You who take pleasure in their words, Guard your coins"

Scarcely had he arrived in Rome than he met some Merchants from Nancy who recognized him and, knowing the grief of his father and mother, forced him to return with them and brought him to his parents.

The homecoming of the boy with a "pleasant countenance" is not described. Felibien goes on to say that Jacques made a second flight soon after the gypsy adventure. The new escapade proved less successful than the first since he got no farther than northern Italy. His older brother discovered him at Turin and brought him home.

After this adventure, a veil of privacy is drawn across that home where the father painted coats of arms and the mother bore many children. The mother's character, for example, remains unknown. It is tempting to think of her as warm and gracious, and of Jacques' father as a stubborn man, although maybe within each parent lay some of the boy's own complexity of nature.

It is fairly certain that life in the Callot household was not routine. For one thing, the influence of the court was interwoven with that of a powerful religion. Those were the turbulent days of the Counter Reformation when throughout Europe the Catholics and their opponents, the Protestants, often embraced their beliefs with special fervor. Most Lorrainers were ardent Catholics. Nancy was not only the seat of the dukes but a city of churches where the bells of Lorraine bellfounders constantly tolled. Of the eight Callot children who grew to maturity, five became priests or nuns.

Of the three children who cast their lot with the world, one was a girl born too late to have played an active role in Jacques' boyhood. Nothing is known of her beyond her marriage to a Lorraine gentleman, to whom Jacques later bequeathed a stud horse.

The eldest son, Jean II, barely missed becoming a priest. He was 16 when he was appointed to the family's benefice at Bainville-sur-Madon. But not long afterward, in 1608,

Europe, 1600. Callot's native Duchy of Lorraine lay between France, the Spanish Netherlands, and the German states which **were** affiliated with the Holy Roman Empire of the Hapsburgs. Lines indicate Callot's overland travels, and the general area of his long Mediterranean cruise during the summer of 1620

he resigned his priestly office in favor of serving the Duke, and eventually he became the family's next Herald of Arms at the court of Lorraine.

✳ CALLOT WINS HIS CAREER

Jacques, in the meantime, won his struggle for the career of an artist. On January 16, 1607, when he was about 15 years old, his father apprenticed him to a Nancy goldsmith named Crocq for a term of four years.

Apprenticeship was the prevailing system under which boys of that time learned their crafts. It entitled a boy to receive instruction from a master in return for helping with routine duties. Jacques, by the standards of those days, was making a late start, but at least he had gained a foothold in a workshop.

Crocq would teach him the craft of a goldsmith. Although the word "goldsmith" literally means a "worker in gold," a goldsmith of that period often did more than make objects of gold. He might, for instance, carve, or engrave, ornaments on steel armor or turn his hand to making a picture on a copper plate from which prints would then be produced.

Engraving pictures on copper appealed to Jacques, but he learned little about it from his master. Perhaps Crocq may not have had much to offer in this field of picture-making. Crocq engraved dies, stamps used in making coins and seals for Nancy, and that is all that we know of him —beyond the fact that he did not retain Jacques for the entire four years of the contract.

Toward the end of 1608, Jacques Callot was on his way to continue his studies at Rome. His means of getting to that city are obscure, but whatever his mode of travel and whatever the routes he took, he carried within him boyhood impressions from his native Nancy—a whole panorama of them.

TWO

Callot in Rome

Rome presented new and varying impressions to widen young Callot's vision of life. His eyes beheld a city hundreds of times bigger than the northern one he had left. The City of the Popes was the capital of Christendom and the crossroads of the known world. Rome, sprawling on seven hills beneath a bright southern sky, offered a spectacle of infinite variety.

The new and the old mingled in Rome, for the Popes had built their city on the ruins of the capital of the Roman Empire, and many of those ruins remained. Here in one street Callot might see the ancient statue of a river god, and in another, the pillared Temple of Venus or the tall shaft rising above Emperor Hadrian's tomb. There were the palaces and gardens of more recent times and Catholic churches galore. The huge dome of St. Peter's, the largest church in Christendom, dominated the city's skyline. Along the busy thoroughfares moved an endless procession of vivid characters. Young Roman patricians and noblemen galloped by on spirited horses. Scarlet and gilt coaches bore red-robed cardinals to papal functions at the Vatican. The clatter of hoofs and rattle of wheels mixed with street cries of Italian vendors and the conversations of foreigners from many lands.

Callot joined an international colony of artists. Others, too, came from everywhere because Rome was the art capital of Europe. Here the experienced artists secured commissions for paintings and works of sculpture to adorn some new construction at the Vatican or at a palace or favorite church of a cardinal, prince, or wealthy nobleman. The student artists learned their crafts in the many workshops. Yet, in spite of the activity in the arts, no one succeeded in filling the void left by Michelangelo, who had created not only the famous dome of St. Peter's but some stupendous frescoes and a masterpiece of sculpture, the "Pietà," a representation of the dead Christ in his mother's arms. Michelangelo, architect, sculptor, and painter, was the last great genius in the powerful movement known as the Renaissance; he had been dead for 50 years.

The most talked-of contemporary artist when Callot arrived in Rome was the painter Caravaggio, whose religious pictures in various churches were marked by a new kind of realism. But not everyone accepted the bold, almost violent style of this painter who had recently been exiled from Rome because of a brawl. Most good artists in 1609 were groping for their own way to capture the mood of the new century.

❋ YOUNG CALLOT BECOMES AN APPRENTICE IN ROME

Callot, who had not mastered the tools necessary for any form of expression, apprenticed himself to an engraver named Thomassin, a Frenchman, who could use the skill Callot had learned from Crocq. Here, in Thomassin's workshop, the boy saw the familiar copper plates, some much bigger than those he had known. Here he smelled and handled that black ink which somehow already appealed to him more than color. He could not guess how far he would one day surpass old Thomassin from Troyes in making black and white glow and sparkle.

His new master had come to Rome 30 years earlier.

Plate 5. Pietà.
Callot's engraving of
Michelangelo's masterpiece
in marble is one of
the Lorrainer's early
"Thirty Views of Rome."
He created this series
while a young apprentice
in the City of the Popes

Though not a truly creative man, Thomassin possessed the technical skill and business acumen to run a successful shop in a city that was a commercial center for the process of engraving. ("Engraving" is the general name for all the different kinds of processes which make possible the printing of more than one picture from a single carved surface. A picture reproduced in this way may be called an "engraving" or a "print.")

In the early 1600's, when neither cameras nor illustrated newspapers existed, prints circulated throughout Europe and supplied the public with the only pictures most people could afford to buy. Prints were popular among both rich and poor. Saints, Bible stories, funeral processions, memorable battles of the past, and copies of famous works of art were favorite subjects. Such prints, reproduced or "struck" from the same plates, were apt to remain in circulation year after year. There was no real effort to give the public up-to-the-minute reports on current events.

Thomassin, in his shop, specialized in the engraving process known as copper engraving. This was the method most commonly used in Europe, and there were no short cuts to its mastery. Callot had to learn the following steps, which were basically what they would be today for any artist wishing to engrave directly on copper:

Engraving a copper plate

1. The engraver obtains a smooth flat plate of copper.
2. To the surface of this plate, he transfers an outline of the picture he wishes to engrave.
3. He goes over the transferred outline with a sharp metal graving tool called the "burin" [PL. 6]. By pushing the burin across the plate, he carves the outline into the surface.
4. He adds details to the outline by engraving directly on the plate.
5. While engraving, he pays close attention to the furrows he has made. They may be of great variety:

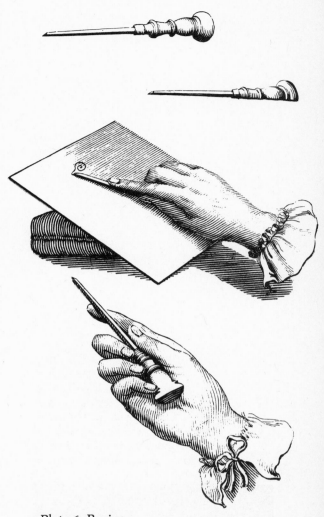

Plate 6. Burins.
This etching by Bosse,
a 17th-century Frenchman,
shows how these tools
are held by an artist
while he is engraving.
During the time of Callot,
an artist would balance
a copper plate on tiny pads
as he carefully pushed
his burin across its surface

thick, thin, straight, curved, close together, far apart, or criss-crossed. They give the differences in tone, the lights and darks, in the picture when it is finally printed from the plate.

Printing from an engraved plate

1. The printer (he may be the engraver himself, or an assistant, or an outside agent) places the engraved plate on a hand press.
2. The printer smears the plate with ink.
3. He wipes the ink from the surface of the plate and allows the rest of the ink to remain in the furrows.
4. He lays a moistened sheet of paper on the plate.
5. The printer manipulates the press, pushing the paper into the furrows. The paper picks up enough ink to transfer the picture to the paper.
6. He hangs up the printed sheet to dry.
7. He obtains a second print in the same way—and a third. And by re-inking when necessary, he can obtain prints until the plate becomes too worn to make clear prints.

From 1609 to 1611, Callot served as an apprentice in Thomassin's workshop, learning a copper engraver's craft. Mastery of the burin was essential. A slip of that tool could ruin beyond repair a clean line on the surface of a copper plate. After a time Callot acquired sufficient skill with the burin to help retouch old plates, an activity that formed an important part of his master's stock in trade. Old plates became worn through frequent printings, and the weak spots on the copper surface had to be retouched with the burin. Callot was also permitted to engrave uncomplicated areas on new plates being produced in the workshop. After some time, with his own hand he engraved entire plates based on pictures by other artists. Finally he added to his master's stock in trade through some very good little pictures that he drew and engraved himself for a series titled "Thirty Views of Rome."

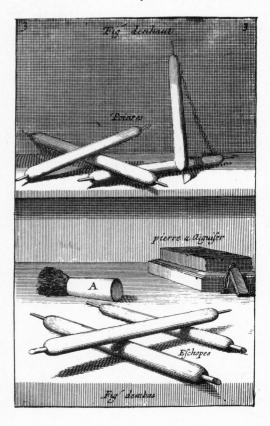

Plate 7. Etching Needles. Here, Bosse shows seven etching needles of various sizes. Callot used fine-pointed needles for his work on copper plates coated with layers of soft varnish

"Thirty Views of Rome" (each of the thirty plates measuring about 4 inches high and 3 inches wide) would give travelers in Rome—those foreign diplomats who came to negotiate with the Pope, or the hordes of faithful who arrived on pilgrimages to holy shrines—attractive souvenir prints to take home. Every plate featured a masterpiece of sculpture or painting in its setting within the Church of St. Peter and in another great church, St. Paul's-Outside-The-Walls. For example, one plate showed Michelangelo's famous "Pietà" in St. Peter's [PL. 5]. This bore Callot's signature, as did many more. It is believed, however, that Callot did not engrave the entire series, which was not published until a later date.

Of Callot's personal life during his apprenticeship with Thomassin, there is nothing to report except an anecdote related by Felibien. He says that the young nobleman of Lorraine eventually fell in love with his master's pretty young wife and left the workshop. Be that as it may, the demands of Callot's artistic development would have required him to move on sooner or later.

A speedier process of engraving, called "etching," attracted Callot. It was faster because the etcher carved his pictures not directly on the tough surface of a copper plate but on a more workable coat of varnish applied to the copper surface. The steps in etching are these:

Etching a copper plate

1. The etcher obtains a flat copper plate and coats it with varnish. (Soft varnish was used at the time Callot first learned the craft.)
2. To the varnished surface, he transfers an outline of the picture he wishes to engrave.
3. He picks out the picture in the varnish with a fine instrument called an "etching needle" [PL. 7]. With the etching needle, he cuts through the varnish to the copper plate. But he does not work directly in the copper. He makes his picture only in the varnish.

Plate 8. Print Shop
for Etchings.
The wooden hand press in
this print by Bosse is like
the one young Callot
toiled on in Rome during
his apprenticeship to
the engraver, Thomassin.
The workers' costumes, however, are typically French

4. The etcher then bathes the plate in acid. The varnish resists the acid. But the exposed copper parts (which make up the picture) are affected chemically. The acid eats into or etches the picture parts, thus making furrows in the copper. ("To etch" comes from an old German term meaning "to make eat.")
5. The etcher removes the varnish from the plate, which is now ready to be printed.

Printing an etched plate

An etched plate is printed in the same way as a copper plate that has been engraved with a burin.

✦ CALLOT, TEMPESTA, AND A SPANISH QUEEN

There was a competent etcher in Rome, a Florentine named Tempesta, whose scenes of hunts, battles, and processions enjoyed wide popularity. Tempesta, who was master of a school and workshop, began to teach Callot the basic techniques of etching. While Callot was adjusting himself to the delicate feel of the etching needle and to the sharp-smelling acid that could bite miraculously into a picture that his needle had sketched in the varnish of a copper plate, an event occurred which put to test the value of all that he had learned during his three years in Rome.

In Spain, in early October, 1611, Queen Margherita died. The death of a Spanish Queen may seem far removed from the fortunes of an obscure, 19-year-old artist in Rome. But Western Europe at the time was a small world in at least one respect: reigning families held many connections with one another through blood or marriage. The late Queen of Spain had been no exception, and she was mourned by numerous courts, including that of the Medici who ruled the Italian Duchy of Tuscany. The Tuscan court, seated at Florence, decided to hold a commemorative funeral serv-

Plate 9. Entry of
Archduchess Margherita
into Ferrara. One of
the first etchings by
Jacques Callot, this work
was included in a
commemorative publication,
"The Funeral Book of
the Queen of Spain"

ice for the Queen in February, 1612. At the time of the service, or as near to that time as possible, the court would issue, for its own private use, a memorial booklet portraying notable events in Margherita's life.

The commission for providing illustrations to be used in the booklet, which was to be called "The Funeral Book of the Queen of Spain," was given to Tempesta. He had worked for the Florentine court and could be relied upon to draw the scenes well and produce plates quickly by means of the etching technique. Twenty-six plates of the Queen's life were needed, and because he did not have time enough to etch everything himself, Tempesta called in a few assistants, among them Jacques Callot.

At last Callot had a hand in portraying some of the human pageantry of his times, the pomp and ceremony surrounding the life and death of a royal personage [PL. 9]. His role, of course, was minor; he was just the copyist etcher of another artist's illustrations. But copying was more than a purely mechanical affair. Artistic taste and judgment were needed, since a copyist had to render the original pictures according to the technical possibilities and limitations of his medium. In these tasks Callot acquitted himself so well that his share in the work took him presently to Florence, where the court would add the final touches to "The Funeral Book of the Queen of Spain" and publish it.

Detail, plate 9

✺ THREE

Florence, a Second Home

Callot was in Florence when the handsome picture biography of Queen Margherita came off the presses there in 1612. It contained 29 illustrations, 3 of them views of an elaborate memorial service held by the Florentine court for the late Queen, and other pictures of episodes from her life. She was seen as a young archduchess riding horseback en route from her native Austria to Spain where she would meet her betrothed. She and the future King Philip III were seen at their wedding. Then came the baptism of their first child, and so the illustrations were presented until the reader saw the Queen breathing her last on her deathbed. Although Callot's contribution to the book was, as we know, merely that of a copyist etcher, good copyists often received credit, and seven of the biographical episodes carried his signature.

The young Lorrainer had reason to feel proud of his achievement. He could also enjoy the realization that his work would reach distinguished circles because the Florentine court, observing a tradition among courts, would send copies of "The Funeral Book" to friendly sovereigns. And herein lay a private satisfaction for Callot: an early copy would certainly be forwarded to the court at Nancy, since the mother of Florence's reigning Grand Duke happened to be a sister of Lorraine's present Duke Henri II. Henri's copy in all likelihood would be brought to the attention of his Herald of Arms, Jean Callot, who could then see with his own eyes that his son, the artist, had made a dignified beginning.

But the old home at Nancy had receded into the background of Jacques' life. He began seeking ways to remain in Florence. He sensed that he had reached a place where he belonged.

THE BEAUTIFUL CITY ON THE RIVER ARNO

Many artists require a second home, a country, or more probably a city, that answers a need within them. In Callot's time, the place for most was Rome, but for Callot himself, the home proved to be Florence, a city much smaller than Rome and far more intimate.

Nature and man had made Florence, on the River Arno, the perfect setting for Callot. Florence, the City of Flowers, had, according to legend, been founded in a field of lilies. These and many other flowers still grew abundantly throughout the Arno valley. It was a smiling countryside of hills and dales, and of trees that gave up oranges and olives, and vineyards that yielded sun-filled Tuscan wines.

The city itself had been the cradle of the Renaissance, that great flowering of the arts and learning which praised the joy of life. During three centuries the city had remained the teeming workshop of Renaissance architects, sculptors, painters, and goldsmiths. Those geniuses took marble and other stones from the neighboring hills and built churches and palaces. They carved statues, painted frescoes, and wrought the iron lanterns and torch holders that helped light the way to an evening's festivities. Callot at every turn saw something vibrant with the beauty that Renaissance artists brought into people's lives.

The Renaissance in Florence had ended 80 years earlier when Michelangelo, the last of the giants, was called by the Popes to work in Rome. The visual arts drowsed in

1612, as if exhausted by the tremendous accomplishments of the past. The names of leading contemporary painters —Rosselli, Poccetti, Biliverti—barely reached the outside world. There were two competent etchers, Giulio Parigi and Remigio Cantagallina, but printmaking as a commercial activity was practically nonexistent. Florence, however, was by no means just a city of memories. Music filled the air, a new music born at the dawn of the new century in Count Bardi's palace where a group of musicians, including Jacopo Peri, had met, played, argued, and created a new form of drama with musical accompaniment—the beginning of modern opera. Callot could hear graceful solos, accompanied by a lute, echoing in the streets of Florence.

People sang in the streets; they gossipped in the streets; they transacted business in the streets. In fact, all classes of people spent as much time as possible out in the open or in their *loggias,* or doorways, enjoying the ever-changing street scene. Events in the streets were enlivened by the extraordinary animation of the Florentines who, over their slightest words, made a point more clear by lifting their voices and waving their arms. Thus, wherever Callot went, he encountered groups of people acting out their lives in the open—in the streets, on the bridges that linked the two parts of the city, in the market places and public squares, and on the steps of the cathedral dedicated to St. Mary-of-the Flowers. On those marble steps sat Florentine dandies with their ornate capes and swords and canes, which the youthful nobleman of Lorraine observed with an eye made all the sharper by his slender purse.

⊞ COSIMO DE' MEDICI, THE GRAND DUKE

The master of this enchanting city was the 22-year-old Grand Duke Cosimo II, who ruled Tuscany and made his seat at Florence. He was a Medici, a member of the family, or the dynasty, which had ruled Florence, with few interruptions, for almost 300 years. During that period, in spite of frequent violence and bloodshed, the Medici had made their name synonymous with patronage, or encouragement and protection, of the arts and learning.

There is a story that tells how, on a day in the high noon of the Renaissance, Michelangelo, as a boy of 12 or 13 years, entered the palace garden of the reigning Lorenzo de' Medici, the Lorenzo nicknamed "The Magnificent." Michelangelo was sketching an ancient statue when Lorenzo discovered him and became interested in his talent. Afterward, the boy lived at the palace and ate at Lorenzo's own table. The story illustrates the personal relationship between the Medici and gifted men. Grand Duke Cosimo II carried on the tradition.

When he mounted the throne at age 19, Cosimo opened his reign with a notable act in support of learning. He gave his patronage to the controversial thinker, Galileo, whose search for scientific truths was blazing a trail in the field of human knowledge. Galileo, a native Florentine, had been forced to flee the land because, while teaching at the Tuscan University of Padua, he had set forth new scientific ideas that antagonized some narrow-minded churchmen. Cosimo recalled him to Florence, appointed him to the post of Court Mathematician and Philosopher, granted him an annual salary, and established him in a villa among the neighboring hills. There Galileo perfected the telescope, enabling man to see the mountains and the valleys of the moon and other celestial sights.

As for the arts, Cosimo extended his patronage to musicians, painters, poets, and other meritorious persons. He liked especially to have them contribute splendor to the public festivals he showered on Florence. These festivals contained fireworks, music, floats, horse ballets, and other spectacular attractions, and Cosimo often performed in them. Of course they supplied evidence for the solemn

Detail, plate 14. Callot found Florence a vibrant and intimate city in which to live and work. He etched this small scene as part of a larger view of the City of Flowers

critics who said that in Cosimo the blood of the Medici showed signs of running thin, and that the burdens of government rested too lightly on his shoulders. But the ruler's admirers argued that Tuscany was at peace and Florence no longer played a heavy role in European politics; why shouldn't the young Grand Duke indulge his pleasures?

This was the slender, dark-haired monarch whom Callot longed to serve. Besides, if an artist wished to make a real career for himself in Florence, he needed to obtain the Grand Duke's patronage. It was unfortunate that in 1612 Grand Duke Cosimo did not require the services of a copyist etcher or engraver. However, this was one more reason for Callot to develop, as quickly as possible, skills that would make him an original engraver—one who produced pictures based entirely on his own compositions. His three years in Rome had been devoted chiefly to acquiring the techniques of engraving. He still lacked training in the elements of picture making—such as drawing, perspective, and design. Giulio Parigi, the leading figure in the arts of Florence, took him in hand.

CALLOT GOES TO PARIGI'S SCHOOL

A bit of the Renaissance, when men of talent were often adept in many fields, lingered in Parigi. He was a good artist, a capable etcher, an architect, an engineer, and the chief organizer of court festivals and ceremonies. He had supervised publication of "The Funeral Book of the Queen of Spain," and could appreciate the quality of the Lorrainer's contribution to that volume. Parigi also liked the young man. An old Florentine art historian, Baldinucci, who published Europe's earliest book about the history of engraving, speaks of Callot's excellent character, saying ". . . since he was spirited and vivacious in his outward manner and even more so in his deeds, he immediately won the affection of Giulio Parigi."

Parigi, among his many other activities, ran a school or academy on the Via Maggio, not far from the palace of the Grand Duke. Boys from great Florentine families attended the academy where they studied subjects ranging from drawing to military engineering. Here Callot began art lessons under Parigi's supervision. They included composition and perspective, which was a representational system that fascinated the Florentines, and drawing, which had always been the basis of pictorial art.

Though Callot loved to draw, he had not acquired the habit of paying close attention to how things were really formed. Parigi advised him to study nature. This meant, for example, that Callot would have to study the human figure and investigate beneath its surface to find out where bones lay and how muscles functioned. He would have to learn how to render folds of clothing, reflections of light on fabric or metal, shadows cast by forms—all this and more he must master [PL. 10].

At first the toil of drawing from nature oppressed Callot. It was Parigi who, according to the writer Baldinucci, helped Callot through those difficulties:

> Parigi, noting Callot's great aptitude for drawing little figures in a mannered, grotesque style, as if he had never drawn anything from nature, did not cease urging him to draw from life. But as it is customary that young people given to this art do not at the beginning of their studies recognize either the final perfections of truth or distinguish between things imitated with cleverness and those executed with mastery and as a consequence much prefer the first endeavors of their ingenuity, that is to say feeble child's play and compositions dictated by caprice, so Callot felt a strong aversion to the discipline of copying nature. Parigi's efforts and affection were nevertheless able to overcome this through persuasion, and without seeming to be oversevere, the master forced Callot through the extraordinary toil of drawing constantly from life.

How Callot managed to make both ends meet during his first three years in Florence is not known, beyond the fact

Plate 10. Seated Man. This wash drawing done by Callot about 1618 reflects the success of Parigi's efforts to make the young Lorrainer draw from life

that he was given some free-lance assignments outside the court. For example, he engraved or etched copies of pictures for the city's handful of book publishers, a copy of a religious painting by the contemporary Florentine, Poccetti, and a huge, ponderous family tree of the noble Florentine house of del Turco.

During these years, Callot kept his eyes on the grand-ducal palace (known today as "The Pitti") which stood at the foot of the Boboli hill near midtown Florence. A magnificent garden stretched up the hill to the Medici stronghold, the Fortress of the Belvedere, where Cosimo's predecessors, who dealt in banking and trade, had stored their vast treasure. Cosimo, having withdrawn from all commerce, was using the fortune to live with the unsullied dignity that he felt appropriate to a family which had allied itself with royal dynasties. His wife was the Hapsburg princess, Maria Maddalena (a sister of the late Queen of Spain). They kept a lavish court to which Cosimo's seven younger brothers and sisters contributed their abundant high spirits.

Cosimo's mother, Dowager Grand Duchess of Tuscany, Christine of Lorraine, lived at the palace, too. (She was a daughter of old Charles III of Lorraine, the Duke of Callot's boyhood.) In spite of her Medici blood, Medici marriage, and long life in Florence, Christine showed little interest in the arts. She was a pious, austere woman who craved political power. But she loved pomp and splendor and, in her sumptuous widow's robes, lent her own touch to the court pageantry of silks, satins, velvets, lace whisk collars, fans, and scarlet hose.

THE DEATH OF A PRINCE

In 1614, a somber event gave Callot an artist's foothold at this court of Cosimo II. Death entered the Medici family during the summer and claimed one of Cosimo's younger brothers. Twenty-year-old Francesco de' Medici, though afflicted with tubercular lungs, had looked forward to a military career and had recently been named commander-in-chief of the army. But, struck down by a fever, he suddenly died. The tragedy affected Callot, and with his burin he engraved a portrait of Francesco [PL. 11].

The engraving was based on Callot's own composition, derived perhaps from drawings he had made of Francesco while alive, or in death, or possibly at both times. It shows Francesco wearing a gleaming coat of mail, and from a high-standing collar edged with lace there rises a proud, curly head and a sensitive face that carries the hopes of youth. Through all this Callot managed to express the court's grief and his own grief over a prince who died too young. The portrait was published in one book that contained the funeral oration and in another that described the funeral services of Francesco.

In the fall of 1614 the Grand Duke expressed an appreciation of his brother's portrait and a recognition of the artist's ability by appointing Jacques Callot as Engraver to the Florentine Court. Callot was 23 years old.

Plate 11. Portrait of Francesco de' Medici. Done in commemoration of the young Florentine prince, this portrait won for Callot the appreciation and the patronage of Francesco's older brother, Cosimo de' Medici

FRANCISCVS MEDICES FERD. MAG. D.
ETRVR.F. OB. ÆT. A XXI.

FOUR

In the Service of the Medici

Take the first room near the staircase, which Signor Giovanni Biliverti now occupies, and which was merely loaned. Clear this out and give it to Jacques of Lorraine, who is going to make engravings for books describing the Life of the Most Serene Grand Duke Ferdinand of Glorious Memory. You will give him such equipment as he may require for his profession, and this chargeable to the Wardrobe.

So reads the court memorandum to an official at the Palace of the Uffizi, where Callot was to be lodged as the newly appointed engraver to Grand Duke Cosimo II.

The Palace of the Uffizi, which had not yet become the famous art museum that it is today, stood on the north bank of the River Arno at the center of Florence. A few private collections of the Medici were stored in the Uffizi, but the Palace, as its name implies (*uffizi* means "offices"), served chiefly for business purposes. The ground floor housed offices for various departments of the government. On the second floor were workshops and lodgings for painters, sculptors, musicians, and other artists who enjoyed the Grand Duke's patronage.

True to the Medici tradition, Grand Duke Cosimo II kept himself in touch with his second-floor protégés. For his convenience there existed a private, enclosed *passagio*, or corridor, linking his palace on the south side of the Arno with the Uffizi across the river. This celebrated corridor, which meandered snakelike for almost a half-mile through

Florence, began its course by sloping gently upward from the palace garden and then, supported by columns and arches, ran over streets and around houses and through the front wall of the Church of Santa Felicità. Here, without leaving the privacy of his corridor, Cosimo might pause in the royal tribunal to look toward the high altar and hear Mass before proceeding. From Santa Felicità, the covered corridor passed along the south bank of the Arno and over the tops of the goldsmiths' shops that lined the Ponte Vecchio, or "Old Bridge," and finally along the north bank of the river to the terraced roof of the Uffizi. From there the Grand Duke could descend into the workshops.

With Callot's workshop there came a room for him to live in. The Grand Duke's patronage brought other benefits to the new engraver: a monthly income; free professional equipment; and the privilege of eating at the table of the ducal pages where, in the gay company of youths from the best Tuscan families, Callot might henceforth enjoy sausages, garlic-flavored ravioli, roasted pheasant, jellies, sweetmeats, cheeses, oranges, melons, honey, and sparkling wine from the vineyards of the surrounding valley. In return for his numerous privileges, Callot was expected to work for the court when his services were required. For this work he would be paid. The court, however, did not intend to keep him busy all the time, and in his leisure hours he might do as he pleased.

✳ CALLOT'S FIRST COURT ASSIGNMENT

Callot's first assignment for the court happened to be a lengthy one. He had to engrave episodes from the wise reign of Cosimo's father, Grand Duke Ferdinand of Tuscany, for a picture biography not unlike "The Funeral Book of the Queen of Spain." The court sent to Rome for copper plates, and when they arrived Callot set his hand to the task. Scenes were to be based mostly on paintings done

33

Plate 12. Marriage of Ferdinand and Christine of Lorraine. This view of Cosimo's parents was engraved from earlier works, and formed a part of Callot's first assignment as Court Engraver to the Grand Duke

by previous artists (including Tempesta, Poccetti, and Rosselli) to adorn Medici palaces, but he had to adapt those compositions to the dimensions of his plates (each plate measuring about 9 inches high and 12 inches wide). Thus, old details had to be changed, and new ones had to be introduced. A few of his scenes are believed to have been composed entirely by Callot himself. In any case, he arranged all of them very well and engraved them handsomely. Of the 16 plates in the series, only one is an etching.

The printing was carried out in his workshop by the staircase in the Uffizi. The court ordered 300 copies of the set. Almost 5,000 sheets, therefore, had to be printed on the hand press and hung up to dry. The court supplied Callot with an assistant and sometimes with two of them, but the responsibility fell on the young engraver's shoulders, and to him goes the credit of seeing a large-scale production through to completion. The prints were published between 1619 and 1620 under the title "The Life of Ferdinand I, or the Battles of the Medici."

Here, recorded officially and solemnly as historical documents, are prints of such notable scenes as the marriage of Ferdinand to Christine of Lorraine [PL. 12], Ferdinand's reconstruction of the aqueduct at Pisa, Ferdinand enlarging and fortifying his seaport and naval base at Leghorn, and Ferdinand's galleys fighting the Turks. In one scene, known as "The Enlistment of Troops" [PL. 13], Callot exercised an artist's traditional privilege and included a portrait of himself.

In this scene, Callot stands with one hand resting on the table of the enlistment officers and bends forward to proffer his talents to the Medici. He gave himself a delicate profile, adorned with a fashionable little mustache and goatee, and dressed himself with elegant simplicity in a well-tailored doublet and loose knee breeches. A nobleman's sword hangs at his side. He bears himself modestly, and the stance of his vigorous, tall body suggests a serious young man moving confidently toward the future.

But that is not entirely how Callot thought of himself when he first began "The Life of Ferdinand I." There exists an early, preliminary study for that final self-portrait. This preliminary study, engraved on the back of one of the plates and never completed, shows Callot as a gay and very youthful courtier. Instead of a plain collar, he wears a ravishing winged affair of lace; the plume of his hat billows like an airy nothing. One would not suspect he ever did a stroke of work. He is all buoyancy, charm, and social grace. Looking at this engraving, one cannot help but wonder about the private life of the young artist from Lorraine.

Plate 13. The Enlistment. In this self-portrait, young Jacques Callot is seen offering his services to army enlistment officers. The print symbolizes the artist's loyalty to Cosimo de' Medici

FIVE

The Festivals of Florence

An attractive young Lorrainer at the court of Cosimo II must have had many love affairs, but no letters or prints suggest any romances for Callot. His four known letters are not romantic and prove him much less at ease with words than with artist's tools. The hundreds of sketches and prints he made in Florence indicate that he must have worked continuously to produce the earliest of those graphic records that won him his place as Europe's first reporter-artist.

As he left his studio workshop in the Uffizi, Callot would stitch bits of paper into sketchbooks to carry in his pocket, and as he roamed the busy streets, he drew and drew—first to practice, then to make notes on characters or scenes to be used in future prints. Naturally, he was absorbed in the outdoor festivals sponsored by Cosimo.

On July 25, 1615, Callot watched the water festival that was held each year on the River Arno in the heart of Florence. This one was called "The Arrival of Love in Tuscany," and it has been preserved in two small etchings by Callot. The first represents Love's ship sending up fireworks from all sides. The second offers a general view of the festival in its setting of river, city buildings, and joyous crowds that line the quays and bridges. Unfortunately, the composition of each plate is weak; details in each could have been more intriguing. Callot himself had eyes to see these and other faults, once his efforts had been completed, but the court found the prints good enough to be published.

❈ A TRADITION OF FESTIVALS

The festivals of the Medici stretched far back in history—
back to the Renaissance when men devoted considerable
energy to the joy of life. Grand Duke Cosimo's rugged ancestors had given festivals to entertain the public and to
highlight their own grandeur.

Cosimo himself took special delight in such entertainment because he was a pleasure-loving prince. Then, too,
because he had weak lungs, his festivals served more and
more to distract him from poor health. They were becoming a breath of life to him, and when health permitted, he
enjoyed performing in them alongside courtiers and professional actors, amateur and professional musicians, and perhaps a painter or an engraver. A single year in Cosimo's
reign brought many festivals: one to mark the carnival season; another to pay tribute to St. John the Baptist, patron of
Florence; another to honor the visit of a foreign prince. All
these spectacles demanded official records, and the records,
if they were in the form of printed pictures, could be sent
to other sovereigns to prove that the festivals of Cosimo II
were the most artistic, the most lavish on the continent of
Europe.

Etchers such as Remigio Cantagallina and Callot's good
friend, Giulio Parigi, had portrayed scenes from Cosimo's
festivals. Callot, borrowing ideas from these predecessors,
added a sparkle of his own, and as the months passed, he
made rapid progress with composition and detail. This progress was shown in his plates of the great torchlight festival,
"The War of Love," held on a carnival evening of 1616 in
the vast city square, Piazza Santa Croce. Prints from the
plates were used as illustrations in a descriptive booklet
published by the court to commemorate this festival, which
was indeed a grand affair. It honored not only the spirit of
carnival time, but also the visit of a neighboring sovereign,
the Duke of Urbino, whose son was to marry the youngest

Detail. African Soldier.
The festival titled
"The War of Love" included
many exotic costumes,
one of which inspired Callot
to etch this gay figure

sister of Cosimo II. Cosimo and his brother, Prince Lorenzo, performed leading roles.

The theme of "The War of Love," as was customary with grand ducal festivals, consisted of a long, rambling allegory about gods, goddesses, and other fictions of the imagination, and served merely as a framework upon which to build real attractions. Callot knew much about the preparations for "The War of Love." His fellow workers at the Uffizi and elsewhere in the city had labored in earnest on the event.

Jacopo del Turco, whose family tree had been engraved by Callot, was in charge of the festival. Del Turco, who shared the Florentine noblemen's love of fine music, had polished up a composition of his own to accompany a dance of masked performers. Jacopo Peri had created melodies that would provide new delights in the evening's entertainment. Poets had written verses to be sung. Lutists, flutists, and violinists had rehearsed their parts. Giulio Parigi had paid attention to the elephants and the camels that would enliven the pageantry, and he had taken care to arrange the beloved horse ballets that would be danced by

Detail. Chariot of Africa. Some heavily laden floats in the festival were pulled by animals, and probably pushed by men hidden near the wheels

Detail. Chariot of Asia.
"The War of Love" featured
elaborate floats, including
one which Callot recreated
in this graceful etching

courtiers riding fine steeds. Parigi's fertile mind had also conjured up strange, glittering costumes, ornate floats, and theatrical machinery that would permit spectacular effects. He had even designed clouds. Florentines could never have enough clouds in their festivals.

On the evening of "The War of Love," the Piazza Santa Croce resembled a boundless amphitheatre. A low wooden scaffolding, erected around the square, held the grand ducal box occupied by Maria Maddalena (Cosimo's wife), and court notables and guests. Innumerable spectators of lesser rank jammed every other inch of space along the scaffolding. The audience, however, extended far beyond the square; windows, balconies, and roofs of nearby buildings were crowded with spectators.

Grand Duke Cosimo and his brother sat on horseback in the side streets. Out there, too, the other participants were gathering in formation. Finally, the various processions began to move, and at their head an oriental queen rode on a marvelous chariot. Her vehicle and the spectacular creations which followed it into the arena are described in an account written for the court's commemorative booklet:

> Above the chariot, it was most wonderful to see Dawn appear on small white, purple and golden clouds. Dawn wore a crown of sunbeams and roses, her costume was white, yellow and bright red. In one hand she carried a brilliant torch, and with the other she scattered flowers incessantly. . . . The chariot entered the amphitheatre escorted by 64 ballet dancers and performers. One hundred and sixty-four Asiatic Indians followed, singing choruses and solos.
>
> After the cortege had placed itself before the Grand Ducal box, there entered an army led by Grand Duke Cosimo disguised as King Indomoro of Turkish India, accompanied by four squadrons of horses and followed by the chariot of the Four Rivers of Asia and by eight giants and many camels. From another side there entered the enemy, Prince Lorenzo, younger brother of Cosimo, disguised as King of Melinda, dark India, and accompanied by elephants and the chariot of Africa, decorated with obelisks. The two armies come to blows in graceful patterns.
>
> The battle is terminated by Venus and Mars, appearing on a chariot which splits into two sections. Mars, on his chariot, sings a madrigal; Venus, on hers, recites a poem in honor of Maria Maddalena. Then choir and orchestra render a concerted piece of music. The procession leaves the amphitheatre and passes through the principal streets of Florence amid the gambols of masqueraders and the clamoring of the crowds.

From this pageantry in "The War of Love," Jacques Callot seized what he could with his etching needle. Three of his plates offer general views of the festival at some moment of its unfolding in the square. One view shows the entrance march of the chief performers into the amphitheatre [PL. 14]. Callot's style is gay and rhythmic, seeming as if he had absorbed the music of the festival and had given it back in his own lively terms. The impact and excitement of the evening is conveyed through the animation of the

Detail. Indian Soldier. An armed Indian was among the fanciful characters portrayed in the Florentine torchlight festival

Plate 14. The War of Love (general view). The Piazza Santa Croce was the stage for the lively city pageant held in Florence during 1616. This print by Callot shows the festival's pattern of performance and also reflects the artist's keen interest in setting and spectators. Typically, the etching abounds in details and small scenes that seize the viewer's interest

spectators who throng the ringside and swarm over the surrounding buildings as far as the eye can see.

Details from "The War of Love" may be seen in another

Detail. Chariot of Mars and Venus. A mock battle during "The War of Love" was halted by the arrival of these ancient gods

print. They are presented separately, each on a small scale and in a documentary manner. Here are Grand Duke Cosimo and the young Prince Lorenzo riding horseback in their armor and plumed helmets. Here is a chariot, and there is a float. But the clouds upon which Love came riding—those clouds most wonderful to see—are absent. Their delicacy is too difficult for the artist to capture. The young engraver to the court of the Medici is still serving his apprenticeship. But what a training ground is provided for him by the festivals of Florence! Above all else, these festivals are helping him find his role as a sharp observer of the passing scene.

During the year of "The War of Love" festival, Galileo, the Court Mathematician and Philosopher known as "The Man of Florence," was called down from his quiet villa among the hills near the city. He was summoned by the Pope to appear in Rome before an ecclesiastical tribunal concerned with suppressing heresy. The tribunal, part of a judicial system within the Roman Catholic Church known

Detail. The Grand Duke. Callot skillfully etched personages who took part in the festival, including Grand Duke Cosimo

as "The Inquisition," had found heresy in Galileo's published theory that the earth was not the center of the universe but a planet which revolved around the sun. Such a theory contradicted the Bible, maintained the church officials who made up the tribunal. The kindly, truth-loving Galileo was forced to declare his theory as false and to promise he would never publish it again. Galileo, of course, would come home to his Tuscan villa, and the Grand Duke would continue to protect him; but the greatest voice in Europe had been muffled. The learning of the new century had received a blow.

At Florence the blow could be absorbed to some extent by the Grand Duke's festivals; their music and pageantry would help to restore the necessary balance of life. The autumn of 1616, the year of "The War of Love" and of Galileo's humiliation, would see another royal visit from the Duchy of Urbino. This visit required a new princely entertainment, and in October the Piazza Santa Croce became the stage for the splendid festival called "The War of Beauty."

CALLOT ETCHES SIX PLATES FOR "THE WAR OF BEAUTY"

Of the six plates etched by Callot and published in the court's booklet for "The War of Beauty," two offer general scenes similar to those in "The War of Love," though sometimes the picturesque spectators are more clearly defined. Each of the other plates gives a detail drawn, this time, on a large scale—and with greater skill. The symbol of Love, for example, is riding with a Court of Cupids and Three Graces on a puff of clouds.

In the carnival season of 1617, Callot tried his hand at recording an indoor festival titled "Intermezzos, or the Liberation of the Tyrrhenian Sea," performed one evening in a hall of the grand ducal palace to celebrate a recent victory

of the Tuscan fleet over Turkish pirates. A general view, the only one the Lorrainer did, shows an elaborate stage of trees, clouds, a mountain, and wee actors far away at the end of the hall [PL. 15]. Little dancers engaged in a courtly ballet are seen in the center of the hall, while around them stand a multitude of ladies and gentlemen, all diminutive in scale. The spectators who are drawn in the forefront of the scene are larger. These are gentlemen of fashion. They dominate the picture, and maybe for this reason the plate, though handsome, was not issued by the court. It is less a record of a Medici festival than a glimpse of high society.

Two other plates, each representing actual details from the "Intermezzos," were likewise rejected, perhaps because they too failed as festival documents. But they were not wasted tasks for the developing artist. He used the experience they gave him for his first great flight of fantasy, "The Temptation of St. Anthony" [PL. 16]. It is a large etching based on that old religious theme, long popular with serious artists, which tells of a saint beset by devils and other grotesque creatures. Here Callot indulged his love of theatricals to such an extent that his spidery freaks, with horns, wings, weird heads, and misshapen bodies, cavort as if they were performing in some huge festival. "The Temptation of St. Anthony" is exciting and artistic. Its lack of religious depth, however, kept the etching from becoming popular at the time it was completed.

Finished with "St. Anthony," Callot turned his attention again to the world close at hand. No more court festival pictures by him were, as far as we know, officially published. His interest in the broad pageant of Florence led him beyond the role of a recorder for grand ducal festivals, and he made quick drawings of gentlemen with flowing capes, peasant women with baskets on their heads, street actors, drummer boys, and others from the endless procession of picturesque characters who passed before his eyes. The color and elegance of the court, however, continued to shape the young artist's tastes.

Plate 15. First Intermezzo. In this print, Callot shows part of a festival celebrating a Tuscan victory over Turkish pirates. The stage set in the distance was made by Giulio Parigi, Callot's Florentine teacher. Titled "Intermezzos, or the Liberation of the Tyrrhenian Sea," the festival took place in Florence during carnival season, 1617

Plate 16. Temptation of
St. Anthony (first version).
This etching portrays many
of the grotesque creatures
which sprang from Callot's
unique imagination. Indeed,
it may take the viewer
time to find the saint,
a tiny figure just inside
the large cave at right.
Completed in Florence during
1617, the work has often
been compared with Callot's
second etching on this subject, done in 1634, near the
end of his life (see pl. 71)

SIX

On the Road to Fame

It was probably not long after he etched his "Temptation of St. Anthony" in 1617 that Callot picked up his burin and, in the exaggerated style of caricature, engraved a little finger-high portrait of himself in monstrous wide-topped leather boots. The sword at his side was drowned in a cascading sash, his tall felt hat topped with a cloud of plumes, and one hand placed lightly on an outsize stick. His face suggests that he is observing the passing scene with a shrewd eye, the eye of a gay dog, a man of the world. One can imagine such a fellow devoting all his hours to a good life in the city or rambling with friends into the flowery countryside to picnic on roast peacock and fine wines.

At that time, however, Callot's workshop in the Uffizi would convey a different story. Here one could find not only remains of Callot's work for "St. Anthony" and the grand ducal festivals, but several completed plates for the laborious assignment, "The Life of Ferdinand I." Prints of "Ferdinand" were already hanging up to dry. Scattered on tables lay sketch books filled with drawings that clamored to be used.

✻ CALLOT'S PRELIMINARY DRAWINGS

Drawing from life had become second nature to Callot, and he drew with whatever was at hand: pencil, crayon, red chalk, pen and ink, or brush and wash. In these quick works he sought to capture the basic movement of a human body, the swing of a cape, the set of a hat, the gesture of a hand. He jotted down the features of buildings, carriages, and other objects that caught his eye. All such drawings were preparatory works; they served only as material for his engravings and etchings. Printmaking was Callot's career.

His drawings, however, deserve a word. By 1617, they were becoming beautiful [PL. 17]. They also possessed the freshness of a thought as it first dawned in the artist's mind. Thus, like the preliminary drawings of other great artists, those of Callot were collected by individual art lovers. A large number of his drawings have been preserved in leading European museums. They have a radiance different from that found in his prints.

Today, fairly accurate copies of Callot's drawings can be made by photomechanical reproduction processes. But Callot, of course, had no such processes at his disposal. With his sharp burin or etching needle, he could not reproduce the soft lights and shadows of a drawing, or the hazy strokes of chalk, or the glowing splotches of wash. He tried, however, to turn his technical limitations to good advantage and make them serve his art of recording the contemporary scene. For example, the abstract splotch of wash in a drawing became, in a print, an area teeming with animated people. But to achieve this excellence, the young man had to discover and perfect new etching techniques of his own.

✻ NEW ETCHING TECHNIQUES

Callot continued to use a burin for "The Life of Ferdinand I," but the etching needle had become and would remain his principal tool. The needle was lighter to hold, speedier, and more responsive to the impulses of his mind and hand as he worked up details of a preparatory drawing that he had transferred to the varnished surface of a plate.

The Lorrainer used several methods for transferring a composition to a plate. One involved conveying a crayon drawing without damaging the original. Callot would place a sheet of slightly moistened tracing paper against the crayon drawing and allow the tracing paper to pick up particles of crayon. The particles furnished him with a satisfactory duplicate. Next, he smeared red chalk on the reverse side of the duplicate sheet and set the chalky side on the varnished surface of his plate. Then, with a sharp point, he went over the lines of the duplicate to give the varnish a chalky impression that would guide him when he drew on the varnish with his needle.

It was the varnish that caused Callot trouble as he developed as an etcher and sought fineness and subtlety of technique. Up to the time of the completion of his "Temptation of St. Anthony" in 1617, he employed a soft varnish used by other etchers. But soft varnish tended to flake at the touch of his needle and to ruin the elegance of his lines. One day Callot tried the hard varnish which the Florentine woodworkers applied to their wood. *Bravo!* No longer did his needle trip as he drew or "laid" his lines. Hard varnish was the answer to the problem of flaking, and the Lorrainer adopted it.

Hard varnish had other advantages. Soft varnish, for instance, had to be used quickly, but with hard varnish Callot could take his time—months, if he wished—over a plate or a series of plates. Furthermore, hard varnish offered stronger resistance to acid when time came to bathe the plate. By manipulating the bath of acid (which, as we know, eats into parts of the copper plate which have been exposed by the needle), Callot before long was accomplishing new miracles. Because the hard varnish was a strong resistant, he could give a plate more than a single bath. He did this by applying a protective coat of varnish to a part of the plate that had already been sufficiently eaten into or "bitten." The rest of the plate then received a new acid bath which bit the existing lines more deeply. The deeper the line, the more ink it would hold, and the blacker it would be when printed. Rebiting was one means by which Callot developed

Plate 17. The Slave Market (drawing). This wash drawing has a radiance typical of many preliminary works by Callot

Plate 18. The Slave Market (etching). The brilliant abstract patterns shown in plate 17 have been replaced by fine lines and details

in his pictures a wide range of tones, the greys and blacks which were his "color."

Callot employed every possible device to achieve his final effects. He used needles of varying sizes. He pressed the burin into service, too, for he frequently touched up an etched line with that tool. Sometimes he would draw with the burin some new detail directly on the surface of a copper plate. Sometimes the details he wished to draw with his burin or etching needle were so minute and fine that he needed a magnifying glass. (The one he used is said to have been given to him by Galileo.) These details usually appear in the background of a picture. They remind us that Callot's prints were destined for an audience that had time to examine each picture slowly, over and over again.

✴ LAYING THE LINES

The first plates on which Callot is known to have used hard varnish were for a series of prints entitled "Various Figures" [PL. 19, 20]. He etched the plates not as a court

Plate 19. Open-air Printseller.
For the title page of his "Various Figures," Callot made this etching of one of the peddlers who hawked popular prints from town to town throughout Western Europe

Plate 20. Man in a
Big Cloak.
This etching provides
one of Callot's models
for beginning artists.
It shows outlines of a
clothed human figure
which have been reinforced
with careful shading

engraver but as an independent artist eager to record the picturesque characters who dotted the Florentine scene. He planned this series as a small book of prints that would serve as a manual of drawing lessons for beginners.

Callot's "Man in a Big Cloak" [PL. 20] demonstrates, with a pair of identical figures, how to draw an outline of the human figure and add shading. The shading is done with parallel lines that taper and swell. This technique of tapering and swelling lines is one which Callot adopted for his own etched work and perfected as his basic method for laying lines on a plate. It permitted him to give a shimmer and excitement to the tones of a print.

"Various Figures," begun in 1617, was not completed until a later date because a drawing manual proved too dull for Callot's mood. He had mastered the art of drawing; he had discovered hard varnish and improved his etching techniques. Consequently, he decided to present his Florentine characters in another series, the "Caprices," more in keeping with his high spirits.

CALLOT PRESENTS THE "CAPRICES"

Rat-a-tat-tat-tat! Here is the first of Callot's lovable drummer boys [PL. 21]. He stands in the foreground of a picture, legs flung apart, head tossed back, and beating his drum for all he is worth. Behind him, like a tiny stage scene in lines often no thicker than a fine thread, spreads the ceremony of "Flag Play" on the Piazza Santa Croce.

Turning the pages of the miniature booklet in which the "Caprices" appear, one discovers another tiny stage scene, "The Festival of the Tribute." In it, wee figures riding with banners around the historic Piazza della Signoria are personages who, in accord with tradition, have come to pay tribute to the ruler of Florence for the lands, forts, and castles they hold as gifts from him. A gentleman spectator standing in the foreground indicates by the cut of his fash-

Plate 21. Flag Play
on the Piazza Santa Croce.
Behind one of Callot's
famous drummer boys,
a spirited contest
takes place in Florence

Plate 22. Duel with
Swords and Poignards.
As Callot's print suggests,
weapons were a gentleman's
valued accessories in
the early 17th century

ionable clothes that this particular festival belongs to the reign of Callot's patron, Cosimo II.

The booklet, which fits in the palm of one's hand, gives many other characters and scenes from Callot's Florence: men dueling with swords [PL. 22], soaring fireworks [PL. 23], bathers sporting by the River Arno [PL. 24]. Views of the Florentine countryside also appear: wild horses galloping on a plain, brigands attacking travelers in a cave, beggars showing their sores. Quiet scenes feature a shepherd with goats, a peasant with a donkey, and a sleepy hamlet where one can almost smell hay in the barn.

The dominant mood of these 50 small masterpieces (each plate was 2 inches high and 3 inches wide) remains one of gaiety and animation, and Callot appropriately entitled his work *Capricci di Varie Figure* or "Caprices of Various Figures." (The word "caprice" is derived from the Latin term *capra*, which means "goat." "Caprice," as a result, has come to signify a goatlike skip or a frolic.) The booklet was produced by Callot as an independent artist in 1617 and dedicated to Cosimo's brother, Prince Lorenzo de' Medici, then about 17 years of age. Young and old enjoyed it.

People who encountered Callot's talent for the first time in the "Caprices" were struck by the artist's abilities: liveliness, grace of style, and an unrivaled variety of skills with the etching needle. These skills rendered so many fascinating, microscopic details that one could not fully appreciate them without a magnifying glass. Here was a unique record

Plate 23. Fireworks on the River Arno. Here, Callot depicts another colorful festival, this one held on the Arno, which flows through the City of Flowers

Plate 24. Ponte Vecchio. In this etching, Callot shows lively Florentines swimming and sporting near the city's "Old Bridge"

of Florence that covered a wide range of life. Those who saw the new work must have wondered where the gifts of the artist would lead him.

Callot himself would have been unable to make a prediction. The "Caprices" had brought him international fame. But at the age of 25 he was still learning his craft.

✻ SELLING HIS PRINTS

Callot published the "Caprices" himself. This meant that he printed the plates in his workshop, from day to day, or time to time, to meet public demand. Two hundred prints is said to be a reasonable estimate of the number he could satisfactorily print from one plate. Hairline details did not last forever. In any case, the orginal plates of the "Caprices" eventually wore out, and a few years later at Nancy, Callot etched a duplicate set to replace the earlier one. There were other times when he etched entirely new plates of some of his popular subjects, complete with all the details. In his wondrous world of copper, varnish, tools, and acid, no labor seems to have daunted him.

In Florence, Callot sold his "Caprices" and other independent works directly to the public. This was common procedure among Europe's engraving profession, and besides, in Florence, no regular print firms existed. Some of his prints may have gone on sale at the city's booksellers, and a few may have strayed into the hands of wandering

print-sellers. In his "Various Figures," Callot shows one of
the wandering sellers, a burly peddlar type who has carried
his prints in a flat basket and set up a booth in the open
where people, young and old, stand gazing at his wares.

In the main, the persons who wished to buy Callot prints
knocked at the door of his Uffizi workshop. These customers included artists who had come to study the monuments
of Florence, young gentlemen who were completing their
education by making a grand tour of the continent, foreign
diplomats, and other distinguished visitors at court—all
eager for souvenir prints to take home. Knowledgeable
Florentines also bought his prints. His biographer, Baldinucci, says: "The value of Callot's work was such that it
was rarely seen in public, for the prints were quickly collected by drawing masters and print lovers and locked up,
as we say, with seven keys in the cabinet and conserved like
so many jewels."

Detail, plate 19

SEVEN

A Struggle with Landscapes

In 1618, the year following the "Caprices," the then famous Callot received a commission to etch several landscapes for Grand Duke Cosimo's uncle, Prince Giovanni de' Medici. How the commission came about, the anguish it caused Callot, and the pressures of his work for both Grand Duke and Prince are recorded in a series of letters unique in the art history of that place and time.

Prince Giovanni was in the Republic of Venice, leading the Venetian armies against the Turks. He had conducted a successful siege against the Turkish enemy in Venetian territory at Gradisca, just over 200 miles to the northeast of Florence. The Prince wished some views of Gradisca to give as souvenirs to his friends. An artist on his military staff, a fellow named Ughi, made a drawing of Gradisca, and the Prince sent this model to his steward, Baroncelli, who managed his affairs in Florence. Baroncelli approached Callot about engraving or etching the model so that the Prince might soon have reproductions to distribute.

Callot told Baroncelli that etching would require time, but he did not specify the length of time. Baroncelli, deceived probably by the effortless air of the "Caprices," did not anticipate any troublesome delay. And since Callot accepted the terms of payment and agreed to etch the pictures not in his workshop but in the privacy of his room (to guard the secrecy Prince Giovanni desired), Baroncelli gave

Callot in f. Ifrael ex. cum priuil. Regis

Callot in f. Ifrael ex. cum priuil. Regis

him the commission. All this, together with other details of the agreement, were carefully reported by Baroncelli in the following letter to the Prince. Callot is "the master."

February 3, 1618

To Prince Giovanni de' Medici at Venice:

I have received the drawing to be engraved and have myself given it to the master who is to engrave it, and have read him the instructions and the letter which Signor Ughi has written me about this matter. After having assured him he was capable of doing this, in the presence of Signor Filippo Sassetti [an assistant of Baroncelli], I left him the instructions and the letter so that during the course of the work he may consult them and execute promptly what he finds indicated and specified therein. He has written to Rome for the copper plates which, he says, will cost from 25 to 30 crowns and meanwhile he will use plates which he receives from the Court and which he will replace as soon as the others arrive. He did not wish to fix a price for his work which, he says, will be considerable, since he must copy the whole drawing and make it ready, part by part, in order for the etching to succeed. But he has asked that I give him 140 crowns on account, and as soon as the work is completed, which, he says, will require some time, the thing being very complicated and detailed, he will do all that he can to please, and the bill shall be settled at the rate of what the Court pays him. I have begged him to work with diligence and above all I have reminded him to work where no one may see him. His professional reputation being involved, there is no doubt that he will do excellent work, and as for the secret that nobody shall see him and learn of this, he has promised me to work in his room where no one ever goes. As soon as he finishes a part [or a plate] he will send it, as Signor Ughi instructed him, to Your Most Illustrious Excellence.

[from Baroncelli]

A LACK OF EXPERIENCE WITH LANDSCAPES

Up to the time he received this commission, Callot had never produced a real landscape. It is true that his little country scenes in the "Caprices" had been a step in this

Plate 25. On the River. This etching is part of Callot's early series, "Italian Landscapes," and was made soon after his Gradisca plates. It gives a placid view of ladies and gentlemen boating on a river near a country estate

Plate 26. The Water Mill. Another Italian landscape shows peasants swimming and fishing. A bright sun enhances the serene mood

direction and that there were landscapes etched by Giulio
Parigi and Remigio Cantagallina to help him find a style.
He had, of course, the original drawing of Gradisca territory to serve him as a guide. But he wished to put something
of himself into the assignment, which in his mind's eye
emerged as a series of landscapes. In his room at night Callot
faced technical and creative problems difficult for him to
solve.

On March 10, 1618, the steward Baroncelli wrote to
Prince Giovanni in the Venetian lands:

> The drawing is still being etched, and the master assures me
> that he works at it every day until midnight. But it is, accord-
> ing to him, a tremendous undertaking and one demanding great
> pains if it is to be something fine that will satisfy Your Most
> Illustrious Excellency. But I trust that by the next post he will
> send one finished plate of it. Signor Sassetti [Baroncelli's as-
> sistant] keeps after him all the time. . . .

Yet, on March 24th, Baroncelli was obliged to report to
the Prince:

> This evening I could not obtain a single plate from the
> etcher. He says the work exceeds anything that can be imagined
> and he does not wish to do it hastily, since it must go to the
> hands of a Prince—and a Prince who is a connoisseur. He prom-
> ises me that without fail he will give me one finished plate a
> week from today, and another the following week, and so on.
> I do not know what to say, except that in truth he labors and
> does not cease toiling at this both day and night—during the
> day on one plate in his workshop and at night on another plate
> in his room.

In the margin of that letter, Prince Giovanni wrote in
answer to his steward:

> I await the engraving with intense desire, because I am tor-
> mented by people who ask me for pictures, and Signor Ughi
> cannot, either because of his age or the time it takes, make any
> new ones; but the prints will satisfy many friends who will de-
> light in the gift. Therefore make haste as fervently as you can.

On March 31st, Baroncelli wrote that he was sending the

Plate 27. Deer Hunt near the Manor. In this lively Italian landscape, Callot shows a small party of mounted gentlemen hunters in pursuit of a stag. They are accompanied by foot attendants and a pack of hounds

first of the Gradisca plates by stagecoach and that the rest should soon be finished. Prince Giovanni, in the margin of this letter, observed:

> The plate of the engraved drawing has arrived—truly good —but I desire speed, otherwise the matter is not worth the trouble.

Within the next few days Callot delivered the second plate to Baroncelli, and then he lapsed. On April 14th, Baroncelli wrote:

> The master has not kept his word. He says he will give me something next week. I remind him of this constantly, and do all in my power. But these artists, it seems to me, do not readily

come out of pasture, and it does not suffice to give them what they ask for; a bridge of gold is needed to make them work, above all when they have by way of excuse the serving of the Most Serene patron [the Grand Duke], such as this artist, who works constantly for His Highness.

On April 18th, Baroncelli sent word to Prince Giovanni that the third Gradisca plate was being forwarded to Venice. The Prince replied:

I await the entire picture, which indeed will soon be no more than money cast into the water, because there are pictures of this everywhere by now, and persons who should receive some from me as a mark of attention are buying things perhaps not so beautiful, but it is enough for them to have a picture of Gradisca. Therefore, if something does not come quickly, I no longer know what to say.

By April 28th, the fourth and fifth plates of Gradisca were being carried by stagecoach through the Tuscan olive groves toward Venice. Then Callot lapsed again.

These letters of Baroncelli, which exist today in files of Medici papers kept at Florence, lift the veil on a harassed young Callot as he struggled to create something beautiful with his first landscapes. After laboring on them at the outset in his room at night, he later toiled more openly by day in his workshop, where anyone could have entered, including the persistent steward.

When Baroncelli did visit, it was in an angry mood. However, overhead prints for "The Life of Ferdinand I" hung drying, and on tables lay unfinished plates for that publication. Moreover, Callot was the Court Engraver, and this was the Uffizi. Prince Giovanni, in addition, was in disgrace at court and had lately been banished to Venice because his free, gay way of living brought displeasure to the pious Dowager Grand Duchess, Christine of Lorraine. Baroncelli contained himself and handled Callot as tactfully as he could—while wishing in his heart another artist had been chosen. The steward consoled himself with the knowledge that Callot was the best etcher for this work, and slow though the master may have been with the Gradisca land-

Detail, plate 25

scapes, those he delivered had more than satisfied the Prince, who possessed the discerning eye of a Medici.

On May 5th, after no new plates had been delivered, Baroncelli again unburdened himself to the Prince:

> Of this blessed etcher I no longer know what to say and I understand how perfectly right is Your Most Illustrious Excellency. I complained of the slowness to Signor Filippo Sassetti and to the etcher himself, who yesterday once more promised me absolutely that by the end of the month at the latest the other plates shall be completed. His excuse is the enormous work which, he says, is involved, and the desire to do well. I do not cease to exert pressure on him, pointing out, as Your Most Illustrious Excellency so well put it, that this is no more than money cast into the water since, due to the slowness with which he has applied himself, other prints have already been published. And always the question of money! He has requested 40 more crowns. I told him to arrange the price with Signor Filippo Sassetti, who will always be ready to pay the remainder due him; and I instructed Signor Filippo to learn what the Court pays him for work done for His Most Serene Highness and to calculate on the same basis. I shall settle the account so that he shall no longer have the excuse of delaying because he has not received his pennies.

On May 12th, Baroncelli informed the Prince that the 40 crowns, referred to in the previous letter, had been given to Callot and, of even greater interest, that His Most Serene Highness, the Grand Duke, had paid a surprise visit to the Uffizi workshop and discovered a Gradisca plate.

THE GRAND DUKE VISITS CALLOT'S WORKSHOP

One's imagination leaps to the occasion. The Most Serene Cosimo II left his palace with few attendants and no fanfare. He entered his private, enclosed corridor which rose from his garden and took him over the streets and the goldsmiths' shops on the Ponte Vecchio, and then along the quay to the roof of the Uffizi. From there he descended a staircase probably to discuss plans for his next festival with his staff of architects, poets, musicians, and painters. He moves quietly, because he lacks the vigor of his ancestors and because he suffers from an affliction of the lungs. But he moves royally, so that when he pauses in a friendly mood at the doorway of his Court Engraver, the presence of the Most Serene is felt. Callot, looking up from the Gradisca plate, sees the brocaded suit, the cartwheel ruff, the long, thin face of Cosimo. There is no time to push aside the plate that ought to have been etched in secret for the exiled Uncle Giovanni. Would it had been a plate for "The Life of Ferdinand I"!

Baroncelli supplies us with the rest of the scene in a letter to Giovanni:

> The Most Serene Prince asked and learned what the plate was and for whom the etcher was making it, and told him to render good service to Your Excellency, a prince who is a connoisseur, and to dispatch it promptly. . . . With such eminent solicitude, the etcher now, in my opinion, ought not to fail in any respect. . . .

Yet even the kindly encouragement of the Most Serene does not speed Callot in the production of those landscapes. In each, he searches for a style of his own, and within the next week he delivers only one new plate, the sixth. Prince Giovanni then demands the seventh, and on June 2nd, Baroncelli writes to him:

Detail, plate 27

> Let me say, in reply to your letter of the 26th, that the copper plate [the seventh] which it requests will, the master tells me, be in no way less beautiful than the last one which has pleased Your Excellency; and the other [the eighth] which remains to be done, if these festivals do not upset things, shall be dispatched within a week, or a fortnight at the latest, without fail, so I am assured by this blessed etcher who has held me, and still holds me, on a leash because of this blessed etching.

On June 16th, Baroncelli breathes a sigh of relief as he reports to Prince Giovanni that the eighth and concluding plate of Gradisca is being dispatched immediately. And as to the final payment, Baroncelli writes:

The master has sought me out and requested 200 crowns for his trouble, which, he says, would have brought more than 300 crowns from His Highness [the Grand Duke]. But from Your Excellency he will be satisfied with that. I have replied to him that Your Excellency, having the entire work before the eyes, can very well estimate what it is worth and that I shall pay him all that is recommended by Your Excellency. . . . He has entrusted to me a letter that I enclose, in which he apologizes to Your Excellency for the delay and for other imperfections in the etching. . . .

In Callot's letter to the Prince, it is amusing to find that he does not apologize for the delay. Instead, amidst the flowery language and salutations of those days, he complains of being pushed and hurried—"the haste imposed upon me," he says, in connection with an affair which has taken four months, long months for Prince Giovanni and the steward Baroncelli. But Callot saw it from a young artist's point of view, and he is not afraid to let his thoughts be known. Further, he, the "blessed etcher" who for so many weeks held Baroncelli on the leash, steps right over Baroncelli's head and asks the Prince for more work in the future:

Very Illustrious and Very Excellent Lord and Very Dear Patron:

As this present work of mine will pass beneath the eyes of a Prince as enlightened as Your Excellency, I have wished to give the utmost satisfaction. But the haste which has been imposed upon me only brings the faults more into evidence. Thus it has seemed necessary to me that, while thanking Your Excellency in this letter, I beseech you to pardon my insufficiency and the numerous imperfections of this work, the first I have ever done in the field of landscape. Accept it as the first born of one of your most devoted servants and cease not to employ me, in spite of its faults; I shall bend every effort to serve you better each day.

As I could not have all the copper plates together at the same time, it may be that one has deeper furrows than another. Your Excellency knows that in this case success, in equalizing when it comes to the printing, is better obtained by wiping the plate more deeply with the rag. May Your Excellency pardon my boldness and the vexations; but blame only my desire to be recognized as your servant, without refusing me another opportunity to serve you, because that for me would be a great misfortune.

If some day I can produce a less imperfect work, nothing would be more in keeping with my desire to remain in Your service, considering the distinction and luster I receive from Your name and Your patronage under which I beg Your Most Illustrious Excellency to take me.

In respectfully kissing Your garment, I continue to pray God to bestow on You the glory which Your great merits deserve.

At Florence, June 15, 1618.
Of Your Most Illustrious Excellency,
the very devoted servant,

Jacques Callot

One more letter exists in the correspondence about the Gradisca landscapes. It is a second letter from Callot, dated one month after the June letter. It gives evidence that, on the whole, the Prince was satisfied with the quality of the artist's work. Moreover it shows Callot was learning that even among such notable art patrons as the Medici one must look to one's payments. He had already received part payment in advance (the exact amount is not clear), but the final settlement was yet to be made. Thus he claimed his due, and to justify the bill he described the effort the work had cost him:

Florence, July 16, 1618

Very Illustrious and Excellent Lord:

I have learned from the most gracious letter of Your Excellency with what kindness you express your satisfaction with my work. I derive the greatest contentment from this, desiring nothing else than to serve you. As this undertaking, with no small fatigue and expense, has lasted four months, I beseech Your Excellency to recompense me to the amount of 150 crowns, including the 100 crowns which I have already received and which fall short of my labors. Excuse my impor-

Plate 28. The Small Port. This waterfront scene from the "Italian Landscapes" depicts typical harbor activities of Callot's time

tunity, for into this work I have put not only my time but my health. In any case, I value your good will more than all the money in the world. In conclusion, I proffer my most humble obedience to Your Excellency, and from God I do implore increasing glories for you.

*Of Your Most Illustrious Excellency,
the very devoted servant,*

Jacques Callot

What happened next is lost to us, nor can any trace be found of the Gradisca scenes that demanded so much from Callot. But there exist landscapes, believed to have been etched by Callot in 1618, soon after the Gradisca plates [PL. 25–28]. These prints offer views of country life elsewhere in Italy. Rendered with ease and grace, these plates give no hint of the effort it has cost the artist to develop skills for rendering landscapes. He has borrowed from the styles of Parigi and Cantagallina, but the sense of freshness and beauty of nature is truly his own. And so is his way of dotting a landscape with small human figures at work or at play. Callot's painstaking struggle with landscapes developed further the young Lorrainer's unique ability to record the world as he saw it.

✳ EIGHT

More Records of Florence

In the world that Callot viewed, there were clowns and actors, and these characters stole into his earliest pictures of Florence. They may be seen lurking among crowds at court festivals and cavorting in the "Caprices." These traveling players often performed in Florence, setting up their stages in a street or square. Naturally they appealed to Callot's eye, and his reports on them give us special knowledge of this chapter in the history of the theatre.

✳ CALLOT SKETCHES THE ACTORS OF FLORENCE

Callot loved to sketch these actors, the males with grotesque masks and hats and broad, flat wooden swords, or the pretty ladies, the dancers, and the clowning acrobats. All participated in a form of theatre known in Italy as the *Commedia dell' Arte*. (The term means "professional, or skilled, comedy.") Circus clowns and Charlie Chaplin, with his baggy pants, are among its descendants.

The *Commedia dell' Arte* had been flourishing in Italy long before Callot arrived, and troupes of the comedians had traveled through Europe, spreading its popularity. Two troupes had received enthusiastic receptions at the court of France. But Callot was the first important artist anywhere to give the *Commedia* the attention it deserved. In 1618 he etched for his own satisfaction a trio of separate, full-length portraits of three of its stock characters: The Captain, Scapin, and Pantaloon.

Stock characters in the *Commedia dell' Arte* were fixed ones that represented basic types of people. The stock characters appeared again and again in different plays. The Captain, for example, was a boastful but cowardly young lover; Scapin was a servant who ran errands and played tricks; Pantaloon was always a ridiculous old lover.

As Callot drew him, Pantaloon appears ridiculous, indeed [PL. 29]. He is smugly dressed, and rather old and bent; yet he tries to give himself a nimble look. He has a foxy air about him and seems to be on guard against anyone getting the better of him—but everyone will. Any person who wears such a long false nose must be fundamentally foolish.

Pantaloon appears again in the background of the same picture, performing in a comedy. He is talking to a young lady on a balcony. A Florentine watching the *Commedia dell' Arte* in Callot's day would know how this affair would end. The lady and her young friends would make a fool of old Pantaloon. In the *Commedia*, the ridiculous old man always lost out.

Every performer in the *Commedia dell' Arte* of those days had to have an agile body. The actors, working on crude boards in the open air, met with competition from barking dogs, crying babies, and other disturbances that distracted the ears of the audience. The attention of the audience was caught and held through the flick of an actor's hand, the toss of a head, the forward thrust of a body, a leap in the air, a tumble, some acrobatics, or a dance. The actors paid close attention to how the stock characters they represented would use their bodies to express feelings such as fear, anger, mockery, or surprise. The actors became masters of pantomime, the art of drama without words.

Callot, too, paid attention to gestures and lively action in all that he portrayed, and while in Florence he continued to

Plate 29. Pantaloon. Callot has deftly captured the gestures and stance of this foolish old lover, a stock character in the *Commedia dell' Arte*. Pantaloon also appears in the background, earnestly speaking to a young lady

Fracischina.   *Gian Farina.*

Plate 30. Fra[n]cischina and Gian Farina. This plate, from "Balli Sfessania" by Callot, shows a pair of vigorous actors from the *Commedia dell' Arte*. Note that Callot omitted an "n" in the woman's name, a practice that was not uncommon during his time

Plate 31. Franca Trippa and Fritellino. These two actors from "Balli Sfessania" wear grotesque masks but dance with grace. The background shows a small episode from the repertory of the *Commedia*

Franca Trippa.   *Fritellino.*

sketch sprightly characters from the *Commedia*. Later at Nancy he used some of these sketches in a series of 24 small etchings entitled "Balli di Sfessania" [PL. 30, 31]. *Balli* is an Italian word for "dances." Scholars are still searching for the meaning of *Sfessania*. Is it the name of a troupe of actors? Is it the name of the place from which this troupe came? Or did Callot invent the troupe and the name so he could be stage director of these little scenes where Scapin, Polichinelle, Fracasse, and other characters express for all time the animated spirit of the *Commedia dell' Arte?*

✳ THE DEATH OF AN EMPEROR

With quiet grace, Callot commemorated in 1619 a Florentine event of a more sober nature. In March of that year old Emperor Matthias of the Holy Roman Empire died in his Hapsburg realm beyond the Alps. Florence marked his passing with one of those elaborate memorial services through which the court paid final tribute to the passing of a great relative of Grand Duke Cosimo II. Callot etched a view of the service, which was held in the Medici family church of San Lorenzo. The magnificent catafalque (an ornate structure on which the coffin was laid), the tall candles glowing, the fashionably dressed people of court, the attendant clergy, and the skeletons standing in corners of the chapel—all are shown in Callot's print.

Old Emperor Matthias as a person had not been great, but through his exalted Hapsburg birth he had acquired the crown of the Holy Roman Empire. Thus he had played a role in a complicated political situation developing in Central Europe. Callot knew a little of what was happening, because in Florence he lived not only among artists, but enjoyed the friendship of government people, including the Secretary of State and the Secretary's assistant.

Emperor Matthias had had no heirs. As a result, before his death the Hapsburg family had decided that the crown of the Empire should go to his cousin, Ferdinand of Styria (brother of Grand Duke Cosimo's wife, Maria Maddalena). Emperor Matthias had also held the Kingship of Bohemia, an elective office which he resigned in his closing years so that Ferdinand might be elected to the Bohemian throne. Ferdinand was elected, but shortly afterward, in 1618, the Protestants of Bohemia rebelled against him because he was a Catholic. The rebellion stands in history as the beginning of that long series of hostilities called The Thirty Years' War, a bloody conflict that reshaped the map of Europe. At the outset, however, what happened in Bohemia seemed no more than a local affair.

But an unusual event did occur in the summer of 1619, the year when Emperor Matthias died. The Bohemians elected a Protestant King of their own, giving Bohemia two kings. Still no one thought the quarrel would spread beyond the borders of the country. The second King was a German prince, Elector Palatinate Frederick V, a young man so gay and unsubstantial that the Bohemian Catholics said, "He will prove but a Winter King, a man of snow, destined to vanish at the first rays of the sun."

Grand Duke Cosimo, if need be, would send a few troops to aid his Catholic brother-in-law, Ferdinand. But what transpired in central Europe continued to be far removed from daily life in Florence. There, during 1619, the old routines persisted among most inhabitants. The court, however, felt the impact of the Grand Duke's worsening health and, doubtless, those who loved him put special effort into creation of the festivals that brought him much momentary pleasure.

"Battle of the Weavers and the Dyers / Festival Presented at Florence / on the River Arno on July 25, 1619" —so reads the inscription on a plate etched by Callot and known today as "The Fan" [PL. 32]. It is his loveliest view of the City of Flowers. The name which has been given to the print comes from the elegant fan-shaped border designed both to frame and form a part of the whole scene.

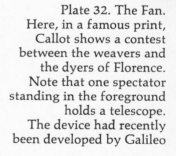

Plate 32. The Fan. Here, in a famous print, Callot shows a contest between the weavers and the dyers of Florence. Note that one spectator standing in the foreground holds a telescope. The device had recently been developed by Galileo

Detail, plate 32

74

BATTAGLIA DEL RE TESSI E DEL RE TINTA
FESTA RAPRESENTATA IN FIRENZE
NEL FIVME D'ARNO IL DI XXV DI LVGLIO 1619.

Jacomo Callot fec.

Fashionable spectators perch on the edges of the borders; crowds swarm the quays and bridges; a pageant moves along the river; the skyline of Florence sparkles in the distance. Here Callot elevates life into something all fireworks and floats, satins and silks, fine coaches, and other exquisite pleasures. He offers a dreamworld into which the viewer may escape from the cares of daily existence. This kind of dreamworld would be developed by French painters of the next century, notably Watteau, in many beautiful pictures known as *fêtes galantes*. Some of Watteau's figures and poses are reminiscent of those used by Callot in "The Fan."

✳ THE GREAT COUNTRY FAIR OF FLORENCE

In the fall of the year of 1619, Callot set to work on Florence's great country fair, an event held annually on October 18th, the feast day of St. Luke, at the village of Impruneta a few miles outside the city. The church at Impruneta possessed a reputedly miraculous picture of the Virgin which, according to tradition, had been painted by St. Luke. Picture and feast day supplied the pretext for celebrating autumn's earthy blessings with a fair. Callot's "Impruneta Fair" [PL. 33], etched during the fall and winter of 1619–1620, as a large oblong picture, approximately 18 inches high and 27 inches wide. The viewer at first glance is struck by the swing and sweep of the fair on its plateau among the Tuscan hills. Then one notes the finely balanced composition, rendered in a harmony of tones ranging from silvery greys to rich black.

After that, the viewer sees the fairgrounds and crowds. People have come from all over: from the hills, from the city, by foot, on horseback, and by carriage. A crippled man on a homemade cart is being pulled along in front where actors are gathering an audience and aristocrats are buying pottery at a booth. There are booths all over the fairgrounds; in some of these, peasants sell vegetables and

Plate 33. Impruneta Fair.
The extent and exuberance
of the great country fair
held yearly near Florence
have been captured in
this etching by Callot.
The artist's handling of
tone and subject matter
makes this print
one of his masterpieces

fruits from their farms. Oxen and donkeys belonging to the peasants stand patiently. Dogs bark and bound. There are sights galore. A criminal is hoisted to the gallows. Food and drinks are served over to the left at the outdoor cabaret. At the far end of the fairgrounds is the church, where knots of the faithful wait at the door while priests display the miraculous picture of the Virgin.

All this and more are in Callot's "Impruneta Fair." Much of the event can be seen with the naked eye; more will be revealed under a magnifying glass. A Flemish artist, Tenier the Younger, painted a copy of the etching in later years, and he said that to match the etching he needed to include in his painting 1,100 persons, 137 dogs, 67 donkeys, and 45 horses.

Callot dedicated his work, which was indeed a masterpiece, to his patron. The Latin words on the plate say: "To His Most Serene Highness Grand Duke Cosimo of Tuscany . . . from Jacques Callot, nobleman of Lorraine . . . in perpetual testimony of a grateful heart." It was a bright gift for a Prince barred by failing health from many pleasures. Cosimo expressed his thanks by awarding Callot a medal suspended from a gold chain. Callot treasured this, and nine years later wore it around his neck when Van Dyck painted his portrait in the Spanish Netherlands.

Callot's "Impruneta Fair" was the result of eight years of labor in Florence. The Lorrainer deserved a vacation, and he chose to take a voyage at sea. In the summer of 1620 he set sail in a galley of the Grand Ducal Navy.

Cosimo took pride in this fleet. The ships were manned by nobles who belonged to the Knights of St. Stephen, a naval order dedicated to clearing the Mediterranean Sea of Turkish and other heathen pirates. Thus Callot found himself in adventuresome company, but a sketchbook of the voyage gives no evidence that he witnessed any fighting. He seems rather to have shared in a leisurely cruise during which the Knights patrolled the western region of the

Detail, plate 33

Detail, plate 33

Mediterranean. As they sailed, touching North Africa, the Balearic Isles, Sicily, and Corsica, he made drawings and watercolors of picturesque old harbors and luminous coasts. After a trip of several months he returned to a Florence that was overcast by a lengthening shadow.

❊ THE DEATH OF A GRAND DUKE

Cosimo was dying. His end might not come immediately, but it would come before long. He had already decreed that upon his death his wife, Maria Maddalena, and his mother, Dowager Grand Duchess Christine of Lorraine, should head the government as coregents until his son, then only ten years old, grew old enough to reign. Everybody knew what this meant. Maria Maddalena had seven other small children to occupy her, and she lacked the strength of character to oppose her energetic mother-in-law. The Dowager Grand Duchess, the pious, austere, and ambitious Christine would rule over Florence. She had, indeed, already taken command.

One of Christine's first steps was toward cutting down her son's extravagance to make way for her own, and she cast an eye in the direction of the artists whom Cosimo lodged in the Uffizi—those artists who had made his festivals and pictures.

On December 27, 1620, Christine wrote to the Grand Master of the Wardrobe:

> You already know that the Grand Duke wishes to reform the gallery [the Uffizi], so you will do well to set your hand to reckoning what should be done in order that the Grand Duke may achieve his aim of reducing expenses to a limited amount, beginning the First of next February. But you should be in a position to do this at least by the middle of next month or sooner if possible. God protect you.
>
> *Christine, Grand Duchess.*

Christine issued the order while her son lay dying.

Cosimo died on February 21, 1621. He received a magnificent funeral, and his body, dressed in a black suit and wrapped in the cloak of Grand Master of the Order of St. Stephen, was laid to rest among the Medici tombs in the Church of San Lorenzo. The funeral oration was subsequently published in a booklet, accompanied by a portrait of him etched by Jacques Callot. The portrait, based on a drawing made while Cosimo was alive, shows him as he looked in his better days—princely, sensitive, alert, and with a twinkle in his eyes.

✺ CALLOT'S FUTURE

Whether Callot was among those artists who had already been dismissed from court service by the time of Cosimo's death is not known. In any event, during the first weeks of the new regime Callot pondered his future. Should he try to remain in the enchanting city where he had been happy?

He had come there as an unformed artist, pressed into no mold whatsoever, and Florence had given him the opportunity to develop his capabilities. In that city, Callot had made a specialty of reporting the contemporary scene, bringing to light the lively and picturesque characters whom most artists had missed. He had also branched out into other fields, and the more than 300 plates he had engraved or etched in Florence showed his range.

His "Temptation of St. Anthony" (1617) had been too fantastic. He had atoned for that in his little "Massacre of the Innocents" (1618), which sold very well, and he was using the same humanized, reverent treatment in another sacred theme, the passion of Jesus Christ ("The Large Passion," 1618–24) which was nowhere near completed. Book illustration, too, he had attempted with success, having learned to grasp the essence of what poets and other writers said. His "Fiesole Destroyed" (1619), "Guide Book to the Holy Land" (1619), and "Soliman: A Tragedy" (1620)

Detail. Portrait of Cosimo de' Medici. This funeral portrait of Callot's beloved patron was made by the artist shortly before he left Florence to return home. The inscription identifies Cosimo as Grand Master of the Order of St. Stephen, and Duke of Tuscany

were proof of that. Undoubtedly, Callot could hope for more work in the future from the book publishers, just as he could anticipate commissions from private patrons, such as Giovanni de' Medici. The question was: could he really make a living and further his career without the assistance of the court?

He had knowledgeable friends, like the Secretary of State, who could advise him. He had his own mind to consult. The conclusion seemed against his trying to stay on in Florence. Where, then, should he go?

Callot could not go back to the City of the Popes. It would be retracing his steps, and besides, he had been bred to the ways of a court. There were other courts in Italy, and at one of them he might find patronage and continue to enjoy life beneath the warm blue skies of the south. In his heart, however, the young man found himself still a northerner, and north of the Alps lay not only Nancy but larger capitals, such as Paris, each with its own court. But why set up his workshop in a foreign town? He was a Lorrainer, his family lived in Lorraine, and he was a nobleman—one raised in loyalty to the court at Nancy.

Callot packed up his belongings: sashes, swords, capes, and the paraphernalia of his trade—prints from his plates, etched plates, unfinished projects, drawings he had used but wished to keep, and countless unused ones that would serve him in the years to come. He did not forget his tools—the burins and needles—and a supply of hard varnish from the woodworkers of Florence.

In the latter part of April he rode out of Florence with the Bishop of Toul, a great Lorraine prelate who had been visiting the Tuscan court on the way up from Rome. They headed north toward the capital of Lorraine, and the Florence of Cosimo's arts and festivals and learning faded in the distance.

Detail. Coat of Arms
of the Medici Family

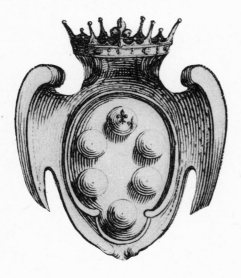

NINE

Nancy Revisited

May, 1621, saw the return of Jacques Callot to Nancy. The 29-year-old artist had won distinction abroad for himself and for Lorraine, but no official recognition by his native land was given to him. Such quiet homecomings are not uncommon for men who make their reputations in foreign countries, and every slighted hero longs for his abandoned field of triumph. Callot's nostalgia for the world he had left was intensified by his love for Florence and the warm-blooded Florentines.

Three months later he wrote to his friend Picchena, the Florentine Secretary of State, and expressed the reluctance he had felt at leaving Florence and his desire to return:

> . . . my departure which took place with the keenest regret and against my wishes, because I never had any other wish than to remain in the most noble city of Florence to serve the Most Serene Princes and likewise many noble gentlemen to whom, as long as I live, I shall remain eternally grateful, hoping to return there some day in the Service, that I may repay some of the great indebtedness I owe. . . .

In the same mail, in a letter to Picchena's secretary, Pandolfini, Callot spoke with even stronger emotion:

> . . . they [the Florentine noblemen] have such graciousness! And the more I see of practices here and compare them with those in Florence, the greater the melancholy that comes over me, so that, if I had no hope of returning there, I believe

I should die. However, a little time is required before I shall be at liberty. . . . On my behalf please kiss the hands of all the pages. . . .

But those happy days in the bright city by the River Arno could not have been recaptured under Christine. Friends there kept him supplied with the hard varnish he needed for coating his plates, and he tried to make a new life for himself in greyer Nancy. He hoped that Henri II, Duke of Lorraine, would grant him patronage. Henri ignored him.

As for Callot's family, it had never been very rich, and there are indications that the fortunes of his father, Sieur Jean, the Herald of Arms, were ebbing. Of the other members of the immediate family, this much only can be said: Jacques' mother was alive; his older brother Jean had embarked upon a heraldic career at court, married a daughter of the Superintendent of the ducal palace and was raising a family of his own; young sister Marguerite had married, or would soon wed, her Lorraine gentleman; the five other young brothers and sisters had entered, or were about to enter, the Church. Jacques strongly needed ducal patronage, but Henri kept him waiting.

Henri lived sumptuously at the palace with his wife (the Italian princess, Margaret Gonzaga of Mantua) and their pair of young daughters. He was generous with his money, but the other parts of his character account for his apathy to Callot. Henri had never possessed the vigor of his sister, Tuscan Dowager Grand Duchess Christine of Lorraine, or that of his father, Charles III, who ruled when Callot was a boy. In his middle years, Henri suffered from declining health and spent what energy he had keeping Lorraine out of the wars that disturbed neighboring lands.

Peace in all areas of life was sought by Henri during this twilight of his reign, and he probably considered it risky to bring into his service an artist like Callot. That fellow was so capricious, so unpredictable, that one could never tell what might turn up next in his pictures. They might not always reflect scenes of tranquillity and the solemn grandeur of the House of Lorraine. Besides, appointment of Callot to the post of Court Engraver would ruffle Court Painter Deruet.

✳ HENRI'S COURT PAINTER, DERUET

Deruet, son of a French clockmaker who had been brought to Nancy by Duke Charles III, was four years older than Callot, but the two men belonged to the same generation. They had known each other as boys and later as art students in Rome. There Deruet developed into one of those artists who, in spite of inferior talent, succeed in dazzling their contemporaries. Claude Deruet had been made a Knight of Portugal by the Pope and then, after winging his way back to Nancy ahead of Callot, had quickly gained the favor of Duke Henri II and become Court Painter and organizer of

festivals. Compared to Callot, he knew little about festivals, and he could not record them, although he held ambitions as an engraver. But Henri was content to let the mediocre Deruet preside over art at the ducal court.

No sign of awareness about what was happening in the arts of Lorraine came from Henri. The arts, which earlier and greater dukes had fostered, were burgeoning and coming into flower. The small duchy had given birth at approximately the same time to three artists of genius who were making their mark. One, the painter Georges de La Tour, was born near Nancy and lived in a town not far from the capital. He worked independently of the court. Another, the painter Claude Gellée (better known in art history as Claude Lorrain), was born in a hamlet in the Nancy region and was down in Italy. The third, Jacques Callot, sought the patronage of the Lorraine court.

Plate 34. Public Square at Nancy. This etching, made about two years after Callot's marriage, shows the city square during carnival time. Among those houses in the forefront at left is one which the artist bought and lived in with his wife, the daughter of a sheriff

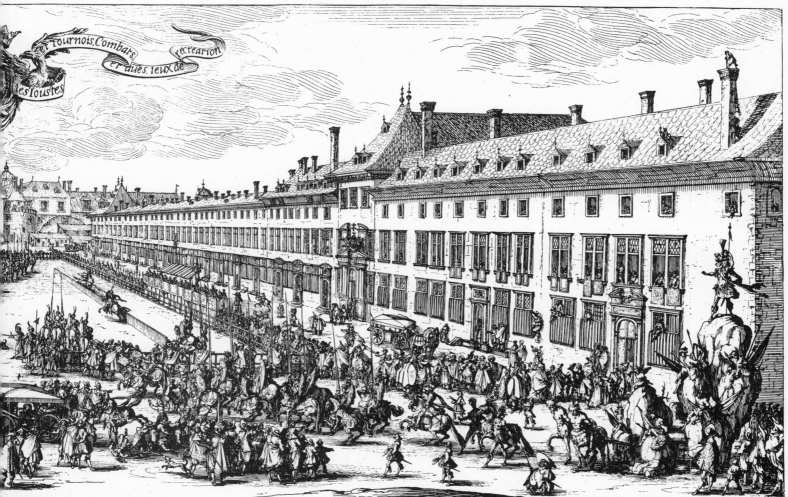

While Henri kept him waiting, Callot tried to establish himself at Nancy as an independent engraver. His location during the first bleak year is not on record. The following year, 1622, he set up modest quarters on a street in the neighborhood of the public square. At some time during this early period of repatriation he sent to Florence for an old assistant, Luccini, who had helped in the Uffizi workshop. Luccini remained in Callot's service for a while at Nancy and then drifted away—a minor talent last to be heard of back in sunny Italy.

✵ FOREIGN TROOPS INVADE LORRAINE

The year 1622 brought calamity to part of Lorraine. Hungry foreign soldiers who were fighting in The Thirty Years' War, then in its fourth year, invaded the countryside in search of food. They could have been driven out only if Duke Henri II took up arms and let himself be dragged into a war he wished to avoid. Henri sat still and let the troops eat their way through the duchy—"like locusts" writes one old historian. The soldiers also laid waste to land and life before they departed. At Nancy, the beggar population was swollen by homeless, starving, and mutilated refugees. Henri's peace, however, had been maintained.

Toward the end of 1622, someone at court managed to obtain for Callot a commission to engrave pictures of German coins whose circulation was forbidden in Lorraine. Almost any engraver could have handled the assignment. The plates were used merely to make documents which would help enforce a law. Callot, moreover, received scant payment for his work, but every little amount helped.

Presently, he moved into better lodgings in a long row of buildings on the public square. The location suited him. The palace stood near at hand, and the square was the hub of the city. In it, tourneys were fought, lords of the court strolled in colored capes and heavy boots, and other characters from different levels of society went about their business. But

Detail, plate 34

Duke Henri, who sometimes rode by in his carriage, remained unmindful of Callot's needs.

Not until the middle of 1623 did Henri realize that this famous man might be forced to greener pastures. Then, to keep him in Lorraine, Henri bestowed on Callot a gift in the form of profits to be derived from crops on various ducal estates during the next three years. The gift attached Callot to the ducal service as Court Engraver. Yet, in fact, Henri still found no employment for Callot's pictorial talents. Court Painter Deruet, at about this time, married the foster sister of Henri's young daughter, Nicole, the heir to the throne. With this union Deruet made another step forward in the monopoly of art at court. But Callot could enjoy the prestige that went with the post of Court Engraver. As for the share in ducal crops, he immediately sold all rights for a good price.

THE MARRIAGE OF CALLOT

Callot was now ready to marry and settle for good in Lorraine. He chose as his future wife a young woman who, like himself, belonged to the lesser Lorraine nobility. She was Catherine Kuttinger, daughter of a well-to-do sheriff in the town of Marsal. The bans, written with the haphazard spelling and other carelessness in documents of the period, were posted on November 11, 1623:

> Feast Day of St. Martin, Nobleman Jacques Calot [Callot], son of Nobleman Jacques [meaning Jean] Calot, Herald of Arms to His Highness, of the Parish of St. Evre, and Gentlewoman Catherine Kettinger [Kuttinger], daughter of Nobleman Nicolas Kettinger, sheriff of justice at Marsal, and she a parishioner of the same place.

Jacques married his Catherine, who probably brought him a substantial dowry. Her personality is not known. His biographers have sometimes looked upon her disapprovingly because in later years, after her artist-husband's death, she quickly married his doctor. After the doctor-husband died, she married for a third time. These facts, however, indicate little except that the lady liked a good home.

Callot's marriage with Catherine proved to be childless—a fact which caused the French biographer Felibien to observe:

> He did not enjoy the satisfaction of having children by this union, but in recompense he had the benefit of producing such a large number with his hand and spirit, these of a kind that will not die, that one may say he left a progeny far more glorious for him than that which many fathers leave in children who frequently do not bring them much honor.

In March, 1624, Callot bought the house where he had rented his previous bachelor quarters. He continued to work at home and to keep an assistant or an apprentice who helped prepare the plates, ink them, print them, and sell the pictures to the public. Customers who came to the little house on the public square included not only local print lovers but travelers who passed through the crossroads city of the north. Callot, despite the lack of official encouragement, had etched constantly during his first three years at Nancy. There were now many prints to see.

Detail, plate 34

TEN

Gypsies, Gobbi, Beggars, and Nobles

If you were traveling through Nancy at the time Callot and his wife were settling in their house on the square, and if you called at his workshop to buy prints, you might not find him in. His apprentice would say, "The master happens to be out sketching, but I will show you what there is."

✳ CHOOSING PRINTS BY CALLOT

The apprentice spreads before your eyes a number of Italian views, including "The Impruneta Fair," printed from a newly etched plate because the old one has become worn. You also see the "Caprices," newly etched for the same reason, and the brand new series of "Dances of Sfessania," based on *Commedia dell' Arte* drawings brought from Florence. But you acquired enough Italian views when you were south of the Alps.

The apprentice brings out some of the master's new religious prints. There is a demand for these in Catholic Lorraine. But you're a Protestant, and now, at the end of a grand tour of the Continent, you are going to England.

You glance at a portrait of Prince de Phalsbourg, Commander-in-Chief of the Lorraine armies. De Phalsbourg, a favorite of Duke Henri II, has had hopes of succeeding to the throne. But the Duke is dying, and de Phalsbourg's hopes are petering out. You pass him up and turn to a lovely

May Day festival at some little village in Lorraine, with musicians playing in a tree. The tree, with its spreading leafy branches, is beautiful beyond words. You're on the point of buying this when you see "The Gypsies" [PL. 3, 4, 35, 36].

Society has cast out these vagabonds, but they are lords within their world. You learn that the master traveled with some gypsies as a boy when he ran off to Italy. How affectionately he portrays them in four sparkling prints, and how knowingly he reveals their mysterious life! What a gallant company of rogues they make as they pass with stolen finery, scrawny nags, and ragged children, or pause to cook a feast beneath a tree—thieves, cheats, fortune tellers, everlasting wanderers, and kings of the open road. Perhaps drawings for "The Gypsies" were made while Callot was working for Cosimo II, but the plates were etched at Nancy in 1621. The prints are for sale. You buy the set.

Then, with your eyes accustomed to what is strange and picturesque, you linger over Callot's "Gobbi" [PL. 37–42]. These are 20 or more palm-sized prints. Unfortunately you cannot afford them all. Which shall you select? The apprentice tells you that *gobbi* is an Italian word for "hunchbacks," and that the master's little hunchbacked dwarfs were mostly etched in 1622 after drawings made at Florence where troupes of *gobbi* performed annually on the feast day of St. Romulus. But you can see that the master has reshaped the fellows into creatures of his own imagination. Some look playful and contented. One, like a wee angry man, thrusts with his sword and dagger. Others clown and dance. Each moves with a grace that induces you to choose five prints showing the *gobbi* making music. Violin, mandolin, bagpipes, guitar, and flageolet have been etched so true to life and with such care that you almost hear the antic music.

Music! How much Jacques Callot seems to love it and its instruments. The apprentice points to a hurdy-gurdy player in a series called "The Beggars."

Plate 35. Gypsies on the Road: The Rear Guard. This is one of four plates depicting scenes from gypsy life which were etched by Callot. The inscription comments, perhaps tongue-in-cheek, on the bravery of these wanderers

Plate 36. Gypsies Preparing a Feast. In another scene, Callot's vagabonds have stopped during their journey to play a game of cards and prepare a hearty meal. The inscription states "In the end, they find it their destiny to have come from Egypt for this feast"

Ne uoila pas de braues messagers
Qui uont errants par pays estrangers.

Callot fec.

bout du comte ils treuuent pour destin
ils sont uenus d'Aegipte a ce festin

Callot fe.

"My master began these 25 plates in Italy," says the apprentice, "and he completed them here at Nancy toward the end of 1622, after those soldiers stormed into our countryside and left many good people without food or shelter."

"Sir," you say to the apprentice, "I have seen beggars everywhere in Europe, and we have plenty of the like in England."

"These of my master," says the apprentice, "show stranger types than you could ever have noted with your own eyes."

The apprentice speaks the truth. Here's a leering ruffian in beggar's rags [PL. 43]; no doubt he and his band rob and murder as they please, but he is picturesque, so you buy him. You buy prints of lawful beggars: the blind man with a dog [PL. 44], and the pair of pilgrims [PL. 45], each carrying a pilgrim's staff and wearing on the hat a cockle shell, badge of the avowed wanderer. Other figures capture your attention, partly because they have been etched more vigorously than anything you have ever seen by the hand of Callot. Cripples, old crones, a man showing his sores, a lovely young girl with a child at her breast—but it is burdensome for a gentleman to think too much about the

Plate 37. Swordsman. One of Callot's "Gobbi," this fellow was chosen from the many dwarfs and hunchbacks who visited Florence yearly

Plate 38. Stooped Clown. Gobbi danced and jousted at the Florentine court on the Feast of St. Romulus, Apostle of Tuscany

Plate 39. Dancing Drinker (front view). Always popular, the "Gobbi" charm and amuse many people who come upon them

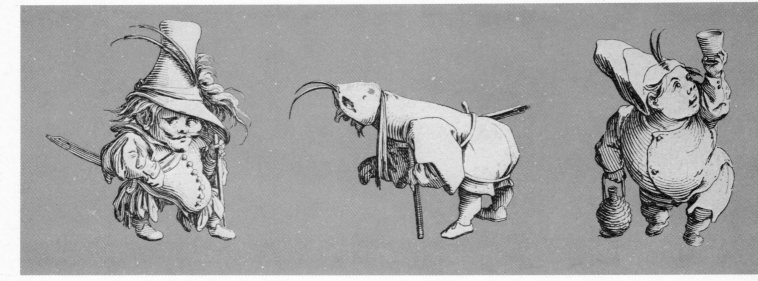

multitude. Besides, you have purchased enough prints.

Then you remember that your host at the inn told you, "Don't fail to see 'The Nobility of Lorraine.' That's what you should take to England. Our etcher is among them. You'll spot him right away."

The apprentice carries out "The Nobility," a dozen plates showing six ladies and six gentlemen. They are a sturdy, well-dressed lot, the men for the most part wearing capes, full kneebreeches and heavy leather boots. One man [PL. 46], however, wears heeled slippers with huge rosettes and gives himself an airy tread and witty face—Callot, of course, and he shall go with you to merry England.

At your inn you pack the prints with care, for the English Channel can be rough, and when you reach London you want to paste them undamaged into the scrapbook that holds your favorite images of the world. You will find, as time passes, that your Callot prints retain their fascination. You have bought some of his most celebrated etchings and will doubtless buy more later on in Paris, for Callot never ceases to survey the world. His eyes roam up and down the highways and the byways to seize upon what no artist before him ever thought would make a picture.

Plate 40. Dancing Drinker (back view). Callot's small men are, perhaps, his fanciful expression of an absurd aspect of life

Plate 41. Bagpipe Player. Many of the "Gobbi" play instruments, suggesting an interest in music on the part of the artist

Plate 42. Flageolet Player. This tiny character plays a flutelike instrument which was popular in Florence during the time of Callot

Plate 43. Captain of the Barons. In the 17th century, every European country had its poor. Callot's "Captain of the Barons" probably led a ragged band of ruffian beggars

Plate 44. Blind Man with Dog. Callot etched this lawful beggar with the vigorous, expressive lines of a new style more realistic than that of his earlier work

Plate 45. Two Pilgrims. These wanderers were part of Callot's "Beggars," a series that influenced several other artists including Rembrandt van Rijn

Plate 46. Gentleman Greeting a Friend. This graceful etching from "The Nobility of Lorraine" series by Callot is believed to portray the artist

The Court of Lorraine

Peace-loving Duke Henri II died in July, 1624, and the court of Lorraine asked its neglected engraver to etch lettering on two commemorative tablets for the double coffin that would hold the Duke's body. For this work, Callot received 40 francs, payment being duly recorded in the accounts of the General Treasurer as follows:

> "To Jacques Callot, etcher, 40 francs for having furnished two copper tablets and having etched on each of these a Latin inscription drawn up by Sieur de la Ruelle, Secretary of State, containing the year, date and hour when the late Duke named Henri II died, together with the years, months and days during which he lived and reigned, with a eulogy in his praise; one of the said plates having been soldered to the lead coffin and the other nailed to the wood coffin of his late Highness, as a reminder to posterity."

Duke Henri, who left no sons, was succeeded by his 16-year-old daughter, Nicole, whose gay, 20-year-old husband, Charles, would help her manage affairs of state. Charles was a nephew of the late Duke, who had viewed the lad with mistrust. "That rash young man will destroy everything," Henri had said. "You will see this after I am dead."

✳ A NEW MOOD IN LORRAINE

After the death of Henri, a youthful spirit began to fill the air in Lorraine. Callot seized upon the new mood and etched one of his loveliest pictures, "The Palace Garden at Nancy"

[PL. 47]. Here is Nicole on a spring day—a tiny, demure figure standing beneath a sunshade with Charles at her side. All the court is with them, playing ball, mingling with gardeners, or merely promenading in an atmosphere which sparkles with innocence. Callot was permitted to dedicate the picture to Duchess Nicole. His work bears the date October 15, 1624.

The opening months of the new regime give further evidence of Callot's improved relations with the court. A handsome, silvery panorama of the ducal capital bears no dedication, but the arms of Lorraine are set in the streamer that carries the inscription: "Public Square and New Street of Nancy where jousts, tourneys, combats and other games are held." It is a carnival scene by Callot, with jousters, acrobats, masqueraders, and other revelers enlivening a dignified square. He also etched a mammoth title page for a physics thesis written and published by Charles's younger brother, Nicholas Francis, the boy Bishop of Toul who attended Lorraine's Jesuit college at Pont-à-Mousson. The plate, crammed with allegorical figures of "learning," is of little interest today except as a memorial to the royal family's one studious member. How different Nicholas Francis was from Charles!

Charles coveted the throne, and in November, 1625, he deposed his wife Nicole on the basis of an old law which decreed that the sovereignty should be held by males of the House of Lorraine. Then he proclaimed his father to be the rightful sovereign. The father, after ruling for a few days, abdicated in favor of the son, and "that rash young man" became Duke Charles IV, sole master of the duchy.

Tall, lean, attractive, restless Charles longed to play a role in world affairs which, in his vision, centered in The Thirty Years' War with its complicated politics and spreading battles. He had been educated in France, but in the early days of the war, when he was only 16 years old, he campaigned in Bohemia with the armies of France's enemy, the Haps-

Plate 47. Palace Garden
at Nancy. Not content
with reality, Callot added
touches from his imagination
to this peaceful scene.
The buildings at left,
for example, did not exist.
Some of the people, however,
were real, including
Duchess Nicole who stands
beneath a sunshade at center

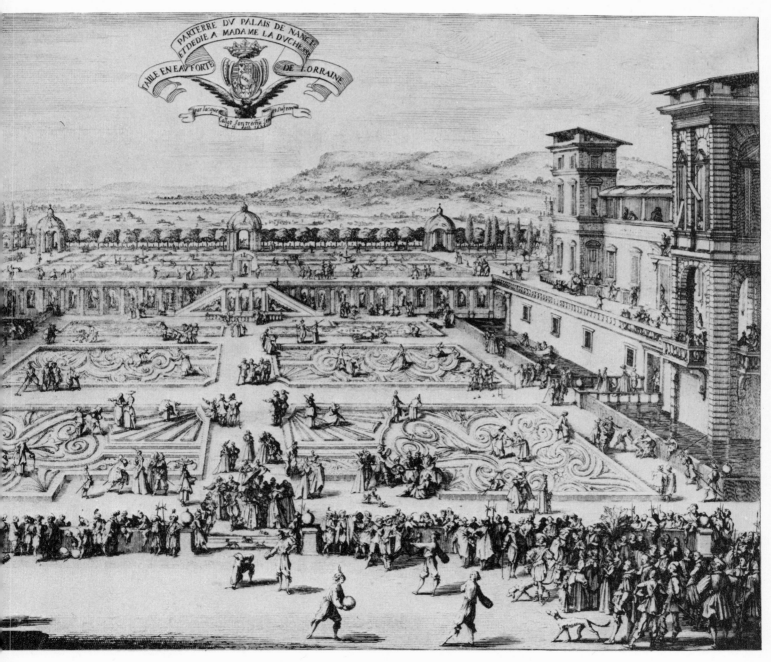

burg dynasty. He still harbored his pro-Hapsburg sympathies and his dreams of glory on a battlefield.

The realm of art did not particularly attract Charles, and he continued the patronage of Callot's rival, Court Painter Deruet, only because Deruet had ingratiating ways and, after all, a Duke must have a Painter. As to Callot's profession, it seems that the only engravings Charles appreciated were those that decorated suits of armor. It stands, therefore, to Charles's credit that in 1626 he gave funds to Callot, the payment of which was entered in the accounts of the Secretary as follows: "Jacques Callot, etcher . . . 2,000 francs which His Highness in his liberality has granted him as a gift to enable him to continue residence in these lands where he has been retained by his late Highness. . . ."

⊞ A DUCHESS VISITS LORRAINE

Soon after he made this payment, Charles was thankful that he had lent support to Callot. In the autumn of 1626, France's celebrated Duchess of Chevreuse arrived at the ducal palace. (The lady is well known to students of European history, and millions of readers have met her in *The Three Musketeers* and *Twenty Years After*, by Alexander Dumas. Her visit to Nancy falls within the period in which *The Three Musketeers* is set.)

The Duchess of Chevreuse was Europe's most notorious conspirator. A beautiful woman, she had been born into a great French family and twice married to eminent Frenchmen. With tremendous wealth at her disposal in 1626, she lived just as she pleased. Love and political intrigue were her chief pursuits, and the more they plunged her into scandalous or hair-raising adventures, the happier she was. Her natural habitat was the French court, but she had conspired in a plot to overthrow French Minister of State, Cardinal Richelieu. Discovering this, the Cardinal had banished her to her brother's home in the French countryside, and from

Detail, plate 47

there she had slipped across the border to accept an invitation to become the palace guest of her present husband's cousin, Charles IV of Lorraine. The Duchess of Chevreuse was 26 years old; Charles was 21.

During the happy days that followed, conversations between the pair frequently turned to politics. The Duchess of Chevreuse possessed a keen mind and a persuasive tongue; Charles made a good listener because he was anti-Richelieu and anti-everything that stood for the rising power of France. The Duchess nudged him closer and closer toward friendships among the Hapsburg bloc, where she herself looked for support against Richelieu and where Charles's sympathies already lay. If Charles had thought twice about such matters, he would have moved more cautiously—but he was never one to trouble himself with sustained thinking.

For the carnival of 1627 Charles planned to offer a splendid festival in honor of his lovely guest. The festival would open with a pageant in which he and his lords, riding on wonderful floats, would pass before the Duchess. Callot, who had learned the ways of the famous Medici festivals, was asked to collaborate with Court Painter Deruet in designing the grand affair. The pageant would be followed by a "combat at the barrier"—a form of tournament in which two contestants faced each other across a low horizontal railing and fought with pikes, swords, or other weapons [PL. 48]. Combat at the barrier had long been a favorite sport with princes and nobles of Lorraine since it permitted them to display their skill and grace. Charles, of course, would enter this event, and the Duchess of Chevreuse would name the victors.

❋ "COMBAT" BY CALLOT

The festival took place in the long Deer Hall of the palace on a February evening, and it was recorded in a commem-

orative booklet, "The Combat at the Barrier," published by
the court. The booklet contains descriptive text in verse
and prose by the Nancy poet, Henry Humbert, and 11
illustrations etched by Jacques Callot. Callot also wrote the
dedication to the Duchess. His prose, stuffed with the gallant phrases of the period, gets no further off the ground
than do the heavy words of poet Humbert, but it does convey some of the atmosphere in which the illustrations were
made for "the understanding of those far away":

To the Very Eminent, Very Powerful and
Very Illustrious Princess, Madame the Duchess of Chevreuse.
Madame,

This Royal House, to which Monseigneur your Husband
[Claude of Lorraine, Duke of Chevreuse] owes the glory of
his blood, has at all times been wont to spend its leisure hours in
exercises which virtue cannot disown. That is why His Highness [Duke Charles IV of Lorraine], continuing the noble cus-
toms of his ancestors, wished, in this present year, with his own
person, to enliven the image of truth with some useful per-
formances. These—for which he honored me with the care of
the machinery, together with Sieur Deruet, whose brush with
its rare talent daily gives a lesson to Nature—have not proved
different from His Highness's intentions. But in order that his
heroic exploits, which shall always be remembered by those
who have admired them, may be brought to the understanding
of others farther away, I have attempted, with my pencil, to
recreate those images, seeking again for them the light of her
who gives it. It is you, Madame, whom France recognizes
as the light of perfections, and who have come to receive the
same tribute from our eyes, our voices and our hearts. We
confess, Lovely Princess, that Lorraine has never witnessed
so many beauties, all the more glorious because they are not
alien. Madame, these are the Heavens where your Sun must
naturally shine to link itself with that great Mars [Charles]
who takes his origin from them. I realize that your mind and
person, being the most notable miracles of Sky and Nature,
can only enjoy matter commensurate with their qualities. But
if so many splendid exploits, brightened by the rays of your
presence, have pleased your eyes, I flatter myself in believing
that the sketches of them may still be agreeable to your mind.

Plate 48. Combat at the
Barrier. In this contest,
recorded by Callot, opponents
faced each other
across a railing erected
in the great Deer Hall
of the ducal palace

I offer these to Your Grace, Madame, with the same reverence that is due to the Divinities, whose effigies live in those of your rank. And since their celestial qualities are openly represented by your own, I await from you the same mercy that is accorded to those who approach their Altars with offering and heart in hand, beseeching you in all humility to authorize my devotion. The favor will be greater than the merit if, with the same eye which your kindness deigns to cast upon the offerings made to it, you allow me to call myself eternally, Madame,

Your very humble and very obedient servant,

Jacques Callot

Unlike these ponderous sentences, Callot's graceful etchings of the pageant [PL. 48–51]—with torchbearers lighting the way, drummers beating drums, and heralds blowing trumpets—take us into the elegant make-believe world of the carnival. The Prince of Phalsbourg, as Hercules, opens the procession riding a chariot on which Cupid perches with bow and arrow. Charles IV of Lorraine closes the procession as Apollo, mounted on a chariot worthy of this sun god. Charles has a cupid, too. Close-ups show the nobles of the land riding on dragons, dolphins, and other fabulous beasts that Callot created with his unique imagination.

Some views show Deer Hall as it looked after the pageant disappeared into the wings and Duke Charles and the lords

Plate 49. Entry of Three Nobles on a Giant Dolphin. In a pageant preceding the Combat, nobles entered Deer Hall on fantastic floats which were later idealized by Callot

Entrée des sieurs de Vroncourt. Tyllon. et Marimont.

Plate 50. Entry of Two Nobles on a Dragon. Beasts, devils, and dragons enlivened the celebration at Nancy, and Callot etched them in his role of Court Engraver

returned to fight the combat. In one view, the contestants salute the ladies; in another, two challengers vie at the barrier. None of these figures, owing to courtly etiquette, are big enough to be identified. Only the text tells that the Duchess of Chevreuse named Charles as victor with the sword and one of his cousins as victor with the pike.

These views record the glamour of a great party [PL. 51]. Tiers along the walls hold hundreds of guests. A box, filled with figures so animated that one can almost hear their chatter, holds the Duchess of Chevreuse. One cannot help wondering who sat with her. The same question arose when the court published the booklet and sent copies to friends abroad. Tongues wagged, and rumors spread from country to country.

At Paris, 200 miles west of Nancy, Minister of State Richelieu knew who the guests were. His spies, as usual, kept him informed. In all probability, Lord Montague, an envoy of England's powerful Minister of State, the Duke of

Buckingham, sat with the Duchess. Montague was at Nancy in those days to lure Duke Charles into an English alliance against France and the tyranny of Richelieu. And surely there were at the carnival other foreign guests who shared in the politics of a Montague or a Duchess of Chevreuse, for Charles had begun to welcome the malcontents of many lands, and his court was rapidly becoming the center of a coalition against France or Richelieu, or both of them.

The Duchess of Chevreuse stayed on in Lorraine another year or two; then Richelieu permitted her to reenter France. "Madame de Chevreuse has ruined Charles of Lorraine," Richelieu was reported to have said. Whether this is true or not, she did leave young Charles well advanced on a political course that might lead him into disaster.

As to Callot, it was shortly after finishing his plates for "The Combat at the Barrier" that he left Nancy to obtain an important commission from another personage of the day, Regent Isabella of the Spanish Netherlands.

Detail. Cupid on a Bird. These fanciful figures by Callot appeared in a booklet commemorating the royal festivities

Plate 51. Entry of Duke Charles IV. After the pageant, Duke Charles returned to Deer Hall on foot. He is seen here as a tiny figure clad in armor and carrying a pike over one shoulder

TWELVE

Making The First Great 'Siege'

With three huge maplike pictures, each made of several parts, Callot became a significant figure in history. The first of these pictures was done at the order of Isabella of the Spanish Netherlands, who respected the Lorrainer as an artist who could report on current events. She planned to use his talent to bolster the prestige of Spain and the Hapsburg dynasty.

When Callot reached Isabella's court at Brussels (about 175 miles northwest of Nancy) in 1627, he found her an intelligent patron who wanted no personal glory. She had often been painted in her jewelled court dress and in the nun's habit she now wore most of the time. Her Court Painter, Rubens, could do that sort of memorial. But the artist from Lorraine had an eye for current events and a skill at storytelling. Above all, he made prints which could be duplicated many times and seen by many persons. Jacques Callot would etch a picture telling of a recent victory won by the Spanish armies when they besieged the town of Breda, a picture story that would be proof of the power of Spain over Dutch attempts to regain independence. Other courts and peoples would see that the new wars challenging the unity of Hapsburg rule in Europe could not succeed. Like Duke Charles of Lorraine, Isabella supported anything that opposed the power of France. Thus, prints of "The Siege of Breda" would also play a role in shaping the political alliances forced upon Europe by the everspreading conflagration of The Thirty Years' War.

At the court of this daughter of a Spanish king, there was a dignity lacking at Nancy. Regent Isabella, a widow in her sixties, was generally respected by her subjects, and foreigners of ability were glad to serve her. Among the latter was the Florentine army engineer, Giovanni Francesco Cantagallina, son of the artist Remigio Cantagallina, whose etchings had earlier influenced Callot. Giovanni Francesco, who had participated in the Breda campaign, supplied Callot with maps of the operations.

✳ CALLOT BEGINS
THE FIRST "SIEGE"

But Callot felt a reporter's urge to see as much as he could with his own eyes and to gather from as many tongues as possible the details of a siege which had occurred two years before he reached Brussels. He was a pioneer in bringing his record as close as possible to an eye-witness account. Printmakers and other artists of war scenes had never shown much concern for campaign strategy or anecdotes of human interest. Callot actually journeyed to Breda (about 60 miles from Brussels), studied the terrain, listened to what the people there could tell him of the siege. "Callot is long overdue from Breda," wrote Giovanni Francesco Cantagallina on July 10, 1627, to a friend at Florence.

Some say that during the period when his Brussels friends lost sight of him, Callot slipped across the border to visit Poelemberg, an artist he had known in Italy, who lived at Utrecht in the Dutch Netherlands (the United Provinces). Be that as it may, Callot turned up again at Isabella's Court before too long, and she approved the plans he submitted for "The Siege of Breda," which in his mind had assumed immense proportions. His final picture was to be a panorama consisting of several sections which, when joined together, would cover an area of several square feet. He would

Detail, plate 55

etch his plates at Nancy, print them there, and ship the finished sheets to the Court Printer, the Plantin Press, located at Antwerp, 30 miles from Brussels. Then Plantin would publish the work on Isabella's behalf.

Callot proceeded to Antwerp to discuss paper, measurements, and other technicalities with Plantin. The city deserved a visit. Antwerp, not Brussels, was the art capital of the Spanish Netherlands. This lovely medieval town on the River Scheldt, 55 miles inland from the North Sea, had once been the greatest port in Europe. Those had been the days when ships sailed up the Scheldt and poured treasures of the world upon the wharves: spices from the East, silks and gold-embroidered cloth from Italy, grains from the Baltic, copper from Germany, codfish from Newfoundland, wines from France, and lions from Africa (for the zoos of northern European sovereigns). A hundred ships or more had arrived daily to enrich Antwerp and support the arts. But the Dutch had blocked the mouth of the river so that no ocean-going vessels might move between the city and the sea. Antwerp had shrunk in population and prosperity. Art, however, is tenacious, artists are tough, and Antwerp kept her place in the mainstream of European art.

A pride of Antwerp was the venerable Plantin Press, located on Friday Market Square, down near the wharves. Plantin was one of Europe's most eminent publishing houses. The present head of the firm was Balthasar Moretus, who is well known in the annals of publishing. Naturally, biographers would like to bring Callot and Moretus face to face. A confrontation of the two experts in the handling of ink, paper, and print would be a shining moment in the history of the graphic arts. But Callot did not see Moretus. Instead, when the etcher went to the Plantin Press he discussed the technicalities of "Breda" with an assistant. Moretus was to make a point of this in a letter he wrote to Callot at a later date, saying, "I did not have the pleasure of seeing you or talking with you in Antwerp, as I was in the printing room and not in the store; you spoke with my colleague, Sieur Van Meurs. If you had talked with me, I would have given you better information. . . ."

✳ THE PRINTMAKING CENTER OF EUROPE

Callot had no reason to feel a stranger in Antwerp. Rather, his visit was to him a kind of spiritual homecoming. Antwerp had been Europe's greatest center of printmaking. Prints from there had directly or indirectly shaped his vision, and those of Breughel the Elder, with their fact and fantasy, had particularly influenced him.

Fashions, of course, had changed, and printmaking in Antwerp was then dominated by Europe's greatest painter, Isabella's Court Painter, Rubens. Though Rubens was not a practicing engraver, he valued black and white engraving as a medium of reproduction. So, under his personal supervision, he kept a group of skilled engravers at work making copies of his paintings. The lush engravings of Rubens' religious, mythical, and other grandiose oils were superb in quality but quite different from Callot's art.

✳ CALLOT MEETS VAN DYCK

Callot found a more kindred spirit in Rubens' former and most gifted pupil, young Anthony Van Dyck. Van Dyck, painter and portrait etcher, was spending time in Antwerp between an Italian tour and his departure to become England's Court Painter. Callot met him, and the two became good friends. It was Van Dyck who commemorated Callot's Antwerp visit by doing a portrait of the Lorraine etcher. The portrait, which may have been a large oil, a small grisaille or one-color painting, or a chalk drawing, has disappeared. Its likeness, however, is preserved in a copy made at the time by the excellent Antwerp engraver, Vosterman.

This engraved portrait of Callot, which appears in the

front of this book [PL. 1], gives a close-up of him at the age of 35, seated before a work table and looking handsome, young of heart, and wearing his fine clothes and fame with modesty and grace. His sharp eyes, which miss no part of the passing scene, have an unexpected gentleness. The medal hanging from a chain around his neck is the precious gift from his old patron, Grand Duke Cosimo II. The capable right hand holds a pencil poised on a sketch for his "Siege of Breda." A loose sheet of paper bears the five stars of the Callot coat of arms. The engraved inscription underneath the portrait reads, "Jacques Callot, Etcher of Nancy in Lorraine, Nobleman."

Toward the end of 1627, after a few months in the Spanish Netherlands, Callot reappeared at Nancy to etch his "Siege of Breda." But the size and importance of this project did not keep him from his habit of working at one time on a number of different kinds of plates. He still found it relaxing and refreshing—as do many artists—to turn from theme to theme or try his hand at some new experiment. Thus in 1628, the year of his "Breda," he etched a number of little masterpieces of a sort quite new to him.

Two of them—"The Card Players" and "The Holy Family at Supper Table"—are night scenes, and as such they stand alone in his work. (A night scene is one in which the light comes from a source of illumination such as a candle or lamp, and in a black and white print the light gives an overall effect of white figures and objects on a dark background.)

His "Card Players" is social history [PL. 52]. Five men of fashion and two charming ladies are playing cards at a candle-lighted gaming table. The setting and costumes recall Callot's recent travels. Legend has it that this is a party given in his honor by Van Dyck and that one of the men is Van Dyck. Anyway, here is Callot having a good time. He is the chap with a raffish, plumed hat and pert little mustache and goatee, who sits cosily between the ladies. This

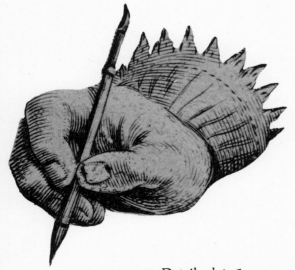

Detail, plate 1

Plate 52. Card Players. In this etching, Callot placed himself sitting at ease beside a fine lady at a gaming table. In self-portraits, he often used devil-may-care poses

pose of a devil-may-care man of the world is one he has often used in self-portraits. To make sure he is identified, Callot has placed before himself on the gaming table, as his wager, a chain and medal similar to the one given him by his old patron, Grand Duke Cosimo of Tuscany.

"The Holy Family at Supper Table" is religious history treated in Callot's tender, reverent, humanized manner, and has long been one of his popular pictures abroad.

A third work, "Light of the Cloister," which Callot also produced in 1628, is a series of 27 little religious "emblems" done for some friars of the Carthusian order to serve as guides of conduct for persons living in the seclusion of monasteries. (An "emblem," which was a popular art form of the period, was a picture expressing a maxim or a fable.) Callot's emblems are beautifully etched in a simple, delicate style, and they portray such scenes as an old eagle losing a feather, Narcissus gazing at himself in a stream, a peasant beating an overladen donkey [PL. 53], and wind blowing a clump of reeds [PL. 54]. Viewing them, a person can feel

110

the poetic overtones which Callot has brought from beyond the fringes of the visible world.

It is probable that during 1628 Callot also plugged away at etching a huge family tree for Duke Charles IV of Lorraine. The tree had to be so loaded with ancestors that even a Callot could not lend it grace. The ponderous, oversize plate deserves mention only as the second and last known work executed by Callot for his young Duke. The brief interest shown by Charles in Callot's art was over, since there were no more festivals to be given at Nancy in honor of the bewitching Duchess of Chevreuse. The Duchess had withdrawn discreetly to another town in Lorraine. From that new refuge, she corresponded with Charles on political matters, awaiting the time when she might be permitted to reenter France.

Because both the Duchess and Charles looked to Regent Isabella for aid in their anti-French conspiracies, Callot's plans to etch the Breda victory caused no displeasure to the Court at Nancy, and he remained the Court Engraver. His personal relations with his Duke were such that in the autumn of 1628 Charles granted him a license to carry a musket and go hunting at Houdemont, where Callot or his wife owned country property.

Plate 53. Peasant Beating his Donkey. Some emblems in Callot's "Light of the Cloister" are fanciful. Others, such as this one, are more realistic

Plate 54. Reeds in the Wind. Here, in another religious emblem, Callot pictured the beauty and grace which he found in natural forces and objects

Detail, plate 55

✳ THE FIRST "SIEGE"
IS COMPLETED

Above all, 1628 was the year when the Lorrainer etched his "Siege of Breda." Regent Isabella had ordered 200 sets of the work, and he printed these and shipped them to the Plantin Press at Antwerp. What route they took by land or river, whether they encountered storms or brigands, no one can say. But like the etcher on his own innumerable travels, the routes of which are almost always nameless, the sheets of "Breda" reached their destination safely. Plantin published them before the end of the year.

Moretus, head of Plantin, deserves special credit for coordinating the many elements of a complicated publication. Seven of his letters to Jacques Callot, though characteristically there are none from Callot, have been preserved in the files of the old printing house, now a national museum, in Friday Market Square. The Moretus correspondence echoes the excitement with which the Brussels court anticipated the forthcoming publication of "Breda." Experts were writing descriptions of the siege, to be set up and printed by Moretus. Some of these texts were being delivered to Moretus by Court Painter Rubens. (A separate booklet in Spanish would tell, in words alone, the story of the siege. It would contain a dedication to Isabella, and the dedication would carry the signature of Jacques Callot, though he was not the author. He had enough to do without struggling over words.)

Callot's picture-story of the siege of Breda contained six separate picture plates [PL. 55–58]. These plates, when placed side by side—three in a top row and three below them in another row—formed one vast landscape covering about 18 square feet of space. Under the bottom row of picture plates ran strips of descriptive text which Moretus had set up and printed separately. This descriptive text was

Detail, plate 55

written in four different languages—Latin (the international language of the educated), Spanish, Italian, and French—so that the largest possible number of people in politically torn Europe might read the details of Spain's victory over the rebellious Dutch. The ensemble of picture plates and descriptive text was framed in decorative borders supplied by Callot. Early owners of the huge work often pasted the separate parts on cardboard or rolls of cloth.

Today, few people get a chance to view the panorama as a whole. People who do have the opportunity will see at first glance a bird's eye view of an immense landscape bathed in light. As one looks more closely, the landscape fades away and there emerges a pictorial chart, or map, dotted with landmarks, each bearing a numeral or letter as a guide to the explanation which may be read below in the descriptive text. Toward the center of the pictorial chart is the town of Breda [PL. 55] and elsewhere a village where the Spanish General Spinola established his headquarters, the windmill where such-and-such an officer took his stand, and the dunes held by another captain of Spain. Scores of landmarks make it possible for the strategy-minded viewer to retrace the campaign in which Spinola and his troops skirmished with, besieged, and finally starved into a surrender the Dutch soldiery at Breda.

Then the picture map fades out to give place to a victory scene where, in the lower righthand foreground, General Spinola, astride his horse and with back toward us [PL. 56], directs Isabella and her entourage as she rides on her way to make her solemn entry into conquered Breda. Isabella remains invisible in her enclosed carriage, but the presence of Her Highness may be felt through the trumpeters who blow their flourishes and the platoons of soldiers who pay tribute to her as she moves through an area now at peace.

Peace, however, has not yet come to the entire region, and in the center foreground, next to the victory scene, there is a close-up of the war zone and an encampment of

SIEGE DE BREDA

Plate 55. Siege of Breda
(complete work). Callot
etched these six plates
to create a single panorama
illustrating the glory of
the Spanish victory
at Breda. The town, sur-
rounded by fortifications,
is near the center of
this vast, intriguing work.
The numbers and letters
scattered on the plates
indicate those landmarks
that are explained in
a descriptive text, written
in four languages and
added to the artist's work

see following pages

Plate 56. Siege of Breda
(lower right plate).
Here, Callot depicts the
victorious General Spinola,
gripping a baton and sitting
on horseback. The carriage
of the Spanish Regent has
just passed in front of him

Plate 57. Siege of Breda,
(lower center plate).
In a myriad of details,
Callot shows the activities
of soldiers in camp and
the hardships of peasants
who must defend their homes

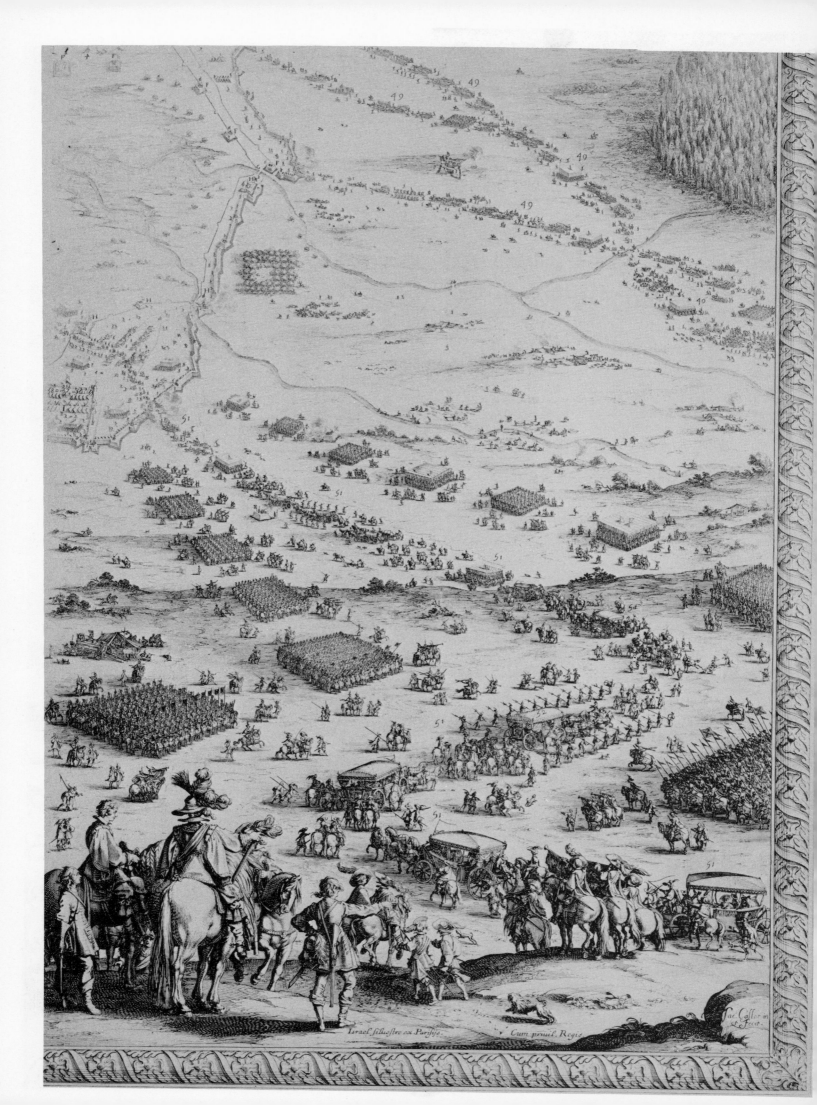

Israel siluestre ex Parisijs.   Cum priuil. Regis.

Scala di passi Geometrici Mille, di piedi cinq. per passo

Plate 58. Siege of Breda
(lower left plate).
Callot has portrayed himself
in the lower left corner
of this plate as a serious
artist interested in
rendering an authentic account
of the Spanish siege.
He again shows the hardships
inflicted on civilians
caught in the battle zone

Isabella's soldiers [PL. 57]. No artist before Callot has shown so vividly and minutely what life in a military camp is like. Officers with swords, sashes, and broad-topped boots stand at ease, while two men by a shattered tree throw dice on a drumhead. Gay, visiting ladies arrive in a carriage, stretcherbearers carry the dead and wounded, dogs feed on the carcasses of horses, a criminal is hoisted on a gibbet, meat hangs from poles at the commissariat, men relax in their tents. The details are absorbing and endless, and carry the viewer to the left side of the picture, where the war goes on. Here [PL. 58], around a hamlet by a canal, Dutch troops are offering their last shred of resistance. They are fighting on a causeway, and boats engage in the combat. Attention then shifts to isolated incidents in which the war ravages civilian life, such as the little scene showing soldiers attacking a hut and killing a peasant.

Down in the lower left corner of this fighting zone is a self-portrait of the artist [PL. 58]. He does not wear that nonchalant air with which he usually presents himself to the public. Instead, he sits firmly on the ground with his sketch book, like a war correspondent gathering firsthand information. Three-quarters of his broad back are toward us, but a glimpse of his well-rounded, serious face is visible under a huge plumed hat. He is a bundle of concentration as an army engineer with a compass bends toward him to give details of the campaign. Yet, obviously the engineer is not the only one the reporter-artist has listened to, or have the army maps been his only source of knowledge about the terrain. He has studied the terrain himself and tracked down all sorts of accounts of the siege, and his efforts have resulted in a picture-story which, with its record of campaign strategy and range of mood, detail, and anecdotes will win and hold a place as the greatest of military prints.

✳ THIRTEEN

Two Other 'Sieges' in Paris

Two more sieges kept the etcher concerned with military history. No sooner had the printed copies of his "Siege of Breda" appeared than King Louis XIII of France, who had recently won the sieges at the Isle of Ré and La Rochelle, summoned Callot to Paris.

The King was fortunate in that his capital had a newspaper, *The French Mercury*, one of the first newspapers to be printed in Europe. *The French Mercury* appeared annually in book form and offered a resumé of leading events of the preceding year, such as the wars that peppered Europe. It gave first place, of course, to the movements of His Majesty, and its pages would preserve the memory of his sieges, telling how at La Rochelle he lived among his troops like a captain as well as a king, and how his magnanimity toward conquered foes proved that he truly merited his epithet, "The Just." But there would be no pictures, except maybe a little portrait of His Majesty or a modest chart.

So the King decided—or his mother decided for him, or perhaps it was his Minister of State, Cardinal Richelieu—that Jacques Callot should be asked to make picture-stories of the two sieges, each to be rendered in approximately the same grand size and dramatic manner as "The Siege of Breda." Then everybody would realize that the King's victories had ended a civil war in France and given his realm new strength for the power struggle among nations.

Callot, exercising his artist's privilege of working wherever there was the opportunity, accepted the commission to etch "The Siege of the Isle of Ré" and "The Siege of La Rochelle." He executed the plates at Paris, during visits he made there between early 1629 and early 1631. Those visits were, in one sense, no more than breaks in his regular life at Nancy, which he still considered his home. But they were to have such a bearing on his career and the course of French art that they emerge as a chapter in themselves.

✳ CALLOT VISITS PARIS

At Paris, Callot found himself in a rich, lusty city with a colorful past and rumblings of a future. Fine coaches splashed through the mud and mire. Peddlars cried, "Oysters! Hot chestnuts! Cherries! Oranges! Lemons!" Gentlemen wore satin or velvet suits trimmed with gold or silver lace. Gallant musketeers, quick to draw their swords and spill a rival's blood, strode around the corners of the street where he stayed with a boyhood friend, Israel Henriet. Henriet had lodgings in the Petit Bourbon Palace [PL. 63], on the right bank of the River Seine, which wound its way through the beautiful heart of the capital. Pleasure boats and work boats plied the river that was spanned upstream by the busy Pont Neuf or "New Bridge." Beyond the Pont Neuf loomed the twin towers of the Cathedral of Notre Dame, bathed in the soft, luminous air of Paris.

Next door to the Petit Bourbon Palace stood the King's Palace of the Louvre. The Court of Louis XIII was the most turbulent court in Europe. Here innumerable factions fought for power, the strongest group being the King's party. Queen Mother Marie de' Medici's party, the supporters of the King's young brother, Gaston of Orleans, and the followers of Cardinal Richelieu also vied for control. The rise and ebb of the various factions are reflected in Callot's work on "Siege of the Isle of Ré." He originally included a portrait of Richelieu along with King Louis. Later, he had to hammer Richelieu from the plate.

When Callot made his first trip to Paris, Cardinal Richelieu, brilliant, ruthless, cruel and ambitious, was seeking to become the mastermind behind the 27-year-old King Louis and then, in the King's name, to humble the powerful House of Hapsburg and make France the first power in Europe. Victories at the Isle of Ré and La Rochelle, victories which had unified France by suppressing a civil rebellion, were steppingstones for him toward his goal. He himself, the warrior in the Cardinal's robes, had planned, waged, and won those sieges for King Louis.

The King loved the excitement of war, but those long sieges had bored him—except for setting up the guns, direction of a few skirmishes, and acclaim as victor. He had relieved the tedium of the in-between moments by going off to indulge his passion for hunting. He cared nothing for his young Spanish-born Queen Anne of Austria or for the charms of any woman. Habit, however, had accustomed him to domination by his mother, Queen Mother Marie de' Medici (a cousin of Callot's former patron, Cosimo II). She was a fat, ornate, and rather stupid person who craved power. Thus, at court, the prime struggle was between Marie and Richelieu for control over King Louis. The King, a sluggish fellow, could not decide between his pro-Hapsburg mother and his anti-Hapsburg Minister.

Cardinal Richelieu immediately followed up the victories at the Isle of Ré and La Rochelle by leading King Louis on a military expedition southward to Italy. The King left Paris in mid-January, 1629, shortly after commissioning Callot to etch the sieges. The main objective of the new campaign was to gain control of the Italian Duchy of Savoy, an independent little state that occupied the same sort of key position on the French border as did the Duchy of Lorraine in the north.

In September of 1629 King Louis's young brother, Gaston of Orleans, who hated both the King and Richelieu,

Detail, plate 59

arrived at Nancy to visit pro-Hapsburg Duke Charles IV. *The French Mercury* admonished Gaston for such a friendship: ". . . You belong to France. . . . Those of the House of Austria [the Hapsburgs] have long entertained a plan to make themselves as powerful in Europe as the Ottomans in Asia. . . ." However, it was not this admonition but new lands and titles from the King which brought Gaston back to France early in 1630. The temporary reconciliation between the royal brothers was a Richelieu triumph which, nonetheless, only paved the way for other difficulties for the Minister of State.

French successes in Italy were followed by reverses. Then, too, a treaty unfavorable to France was signed with the Hapsburg Emperor because, during part of the summer and autumn, King Louis lay desperately ill of a fever at the French town of Lyon and could not issue instructions to his envoys. The treaty so disturbed Richelieu that he told a Venetian ambassador he meant to enter a monastery.

Soon, for a different reason, Richelieu came even closer to retirement. This happened when the King, recovered from his illness, came back to Paris and found Queen Mother Marie determined that he should drive out the Cardinal. The King told her that the time had not yet come to discharge a minister whose services were greatly needed. Marie then made up her mind to force her son into choosing between his mother and his Minister. Her chance came on November 11, 1630.

✳ THE FRENCH KING MAKES A DIFFICULT DECISION

On that day, which was to become famous in French history as the "Day of Dupes," Louis visited his mother while she was dressing in her chambers at the Luxembourg Palace. Cardinal Richelieu happened to enter to offer her his humble compliments. She angrily told Richelieu he was deceiving the King and betraying the state for his own glory, and she forbade him to appear in her presence again.

The Cardinal departed, and the King, after scolding his mother, returned to his own apartments and threw himself down on his bed in such agitation that the buttons on his doublet jumped to the floor. He realized that he must exclude either his mother or his Minister from affairs of state. Louis decided in favor of the one he needed most: his Minister, Cardinal Richelieu.

Marie was banished from Paris and imprisoned in a castle at Blois. She eventually escaped from there and reached the Spanish Netherlands, where Regent Isabella received her warmly and advised her to continue plotting with Gaston of Orleans and other malcontents against Richelieu and France. Marie followed that advice. The King never pardoned her, and years later she died in exile.

Richelieu emerged from the Day of Dupes as master of France, and could finally guide the country along the historic course he had set with the sieges of the Isle of Ré and La Rochelle, which had consolidated the nation. Thus Callot's picture-stories of the two sieges struck a chord in a dawning national consciousness. He completed his etching of both works in Paris toward the end of 1630, and not long afterward they were printed and published by the court. Military and naval authorities in Paris had supplied Callot with documentary information, and probably he made the 250-mile journey to the west coast of France to study the theatre of the sieges and get the feel of ships and the sea. Early copies of his "Isle of Ré" were accompanied by an announcement saying: "Such is the Isle of Ré, which Callot of Lorraine has presented with as much integrity and accuracy as delicacy and charm."

Actually, in human interest and in range of mood his "Isle of Ré" is less substantial than his earlier "Siege of Breda," but it contains fascinating views of the besieged ocean island and Frenchmen loading and unloading sloops and toting army supplies [PL. 59, 60]. The sequel, "La Ro-

Plate 59. Siege of the Isle of Ré (lower left plate). King Louis of France, holding his commander's baton, is seen here with his brother, Gaston. Callot has placed them among French troops who are busy hauling battle supplies and boarding their sloops. The citadel of St. Martin on the tiny island was held by French Huguenots and English soldiers

chelle," although it highlights some memorable fighting ships in full sail, shows a further decline in content and is more like a decorative map [PL. 61, 62].

Callot's hand did not etch every last inch of these two sieges. His work on them was interrupted in August, 1630, when his father's death took him back to Nancy for a while. A Paris etcher, Abraham Bosse, may have contributed to the plates; certainly another Frenchman, Michel Lasne, etched some of the portraits in the borders of "Isle of Ré."

Still, the concepts and the major etching of both sieges were Jacques Callot's, and if he was growing weary of huge victory pictures, the French pardoned him, for by any standards his "Isle of Ré" and "La Rochelle" are marvelous pictorial records. The French regard them as thrilling pages in the nation's history. Today in Paris, handsome, full-size reproductions of old copies can be bought at the Museum of the Louvre, the palace where King Louis lived.

✳ OTHER TIES WITH FRANCE

The French love Callot for other reasons, also. They consider him the father of French etching. When Callot went to Paris in 1629, the arts in the capital were just beginning to catch up with the stride of a new era. During 1622 and 1625, Rubens of Antwerp had spurred them on by painting a vast cycle of the life of Queen Mother Marie de' Medici to decorate the walls of her Luxembourg Palace. In 1627, King Louis brought from Italy a young Frenchman named Simon Vouet (who was fairly good at painting religious and allegorical themes) and attached him to the court. The talented Brussels-born painter, Philippe de Champaigne, who had come to Paris in 1621 and served for a while as Painter to Queen Mother Marie, was now producing fine portraits and religious pictures.

But not much had happened in the field of engraving on copper (either with the burin or the etching needle). The

Plate 60. Siege of the Isle of Ré (lower center plate). In this print, sloops of the French forces sail off toward the English fleet which they eventually defeated. The defenders on the Isle of Ré finally surrendered after a two-year siege

127

Plate 61. Siege of La Rochelle (complete work). After their victory at the Isle of Ré, the French attacked the seaport of La Rochelle. Callot's six plates illustrate their strategy in besieging the famous walled town, which was situated on an ocean creek. At the center of the work is seen the huge mole, or barrier, built by the French to seal off the harbor. Two centuries later, Alexandre Dumas described the siege in his novel, *The Three Musketeers*. Dumas gave his heroes the attitudes of gay adventurers, but for the inhabitants of La Rochelle, the long, bloody siege was a grim experience

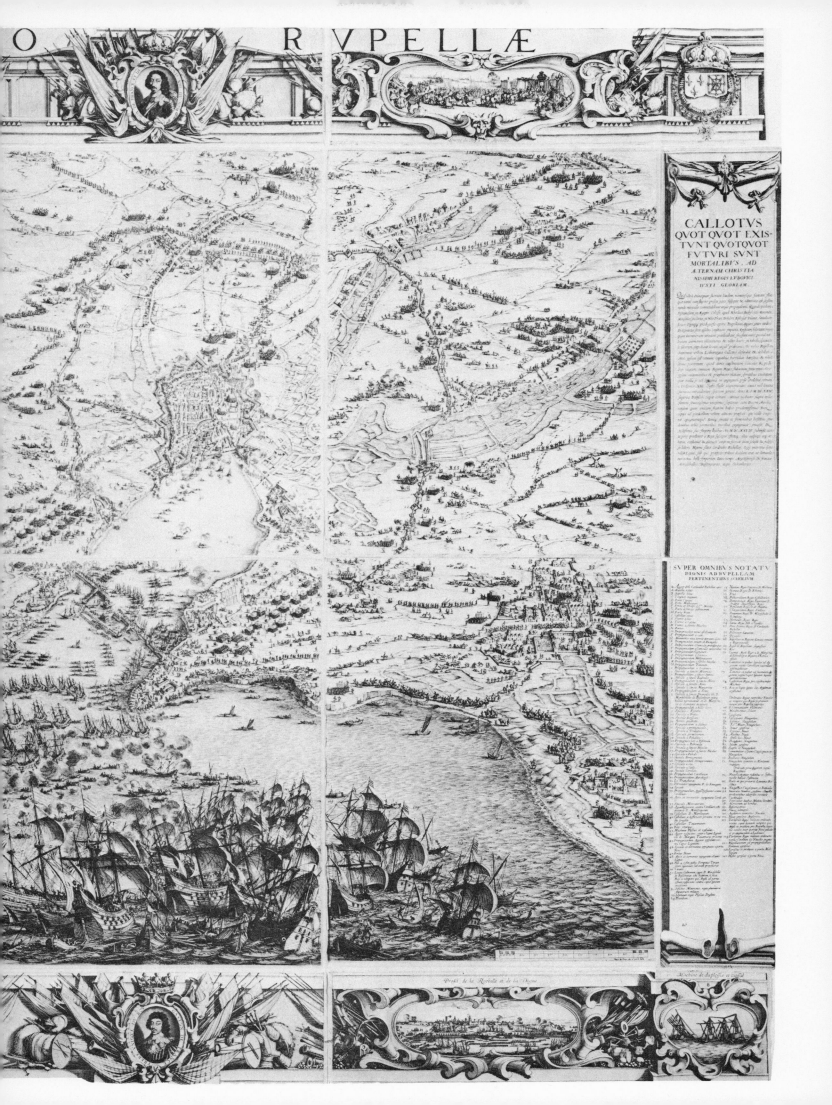

50-year-old Paris firm of Tavernier, founded by a print-maker from the Netherlands, was privileged to use the title of Engraver and Etcher to King Louis XIII, but had been put to no outstanding service at court. Occasionally, Tavernier supplied one of the little folding maps used in *The French Mercury;* they were no more than simple documents. In fact, Tavernier functioned chiefly as a dealer in prints, many of them imported from the Netherlands. Michel Lasne, a French engraver somewhat older than Callot, was competent, but not a genius.

A bright hope for engraving lay in the gifted young French etcher, Abraham Bosse, who, having come recently to Paris from Tours, stood at the threshold of his career. Bosse, still in his mid-twenties, met Callot and a friendship sprang up between the young man and the older one. In later years, Bosse, who had fulfilled his early promise and achieved fame, wrote several art books in which he seems never to exhaust his feeling of affection and gratitude toward Callot of Lorraine. In one volume Bosse speaks of Callot as a kind and generous friend: "The late Monsieur Callot told me that he used a prepared varnish sent to him from Italy. This is made there by wood-workers, who use it for varnishing their wood. It is called Vernice *grosso da lignaiolo.* He gave me some which I have employed for a long time."

In another volume Bosse praises Callot the artist: ". . . J. Callot of Nancy, who produced such excellent work, particularly in small size, which was his specialty, that no one before him or till now has done better; let this be said in his memory, since in this kind of work he almost surpassed what the spirit of man can hope for, and which is partly the reason why at the present we have here [in Paris] and in various other places excellent men in this Art."

And elsewhere, to correct the impression that Callot's talent was limited to small pictures, Bosse declares: "He also etched some large ones as vigorously as could be."

Plate 62. Siege of La Rochelle (lower left plate). Here Callot depicts gallant fighting ships attacking fortified positions set up near La Rochelle. The siege lasted one year, until starvation forced the defenders to yield

131

✳ CALLOT AND HIS PUBLISHER, HENRIET OF PARIS

The French also have affection for Callot because back in the days when Callot and Bosse talked shop along the banks of the Seine, the father of French etching decided, with characteristic flair, that the French capital should become a publishing center for some of his future work. His publisher would be his friend and host, Israel Henriet. Henriet had known Callot not only when the two were boys at Nancy, but also in Rome, where the publisher had studied painting. As a painter he possessed no very special talent, and after coming to Paris and working for a now forgotten First Painter to Queen Mother Marie de' Medici, he gave up painting for etching and developed a knack for drawing with pen and ink. News of this facility with pen and ink reached the ears of young King Louis XIII, and His Majesty decided to embark on lessons with Henriet in the pen and ink technique.

Lords of the court followed the royal example and studied with Henriet until one fine day the King grew bored with pen and ink and turned to pastel lessons under Simon Vouet. Again the lords followed in the royal footsteps, and Henriet, having lost his pupils, decided to earn his livelihood by selling prints that would include pictures by artists other than himself. As one who kept up his contacts in high circles, he was well-prepared to become a print dealer.

The original agreement between Henriet and Callot stipulated that the etcher provide the dealer annually with a number of new plates. Henriet was to "bring these to light" or, as we would say, "publish them." This meant Henriet would pull the prints (i.e., print the sheets from the plates), make their existence known, and sell them. The agreement remained in effect during Callot's lifetime, and Henriet found a ready market for the work of Lorraine's distinguished etcher not only at court but elsewhere in the city.

Paris flourished under the vigorous national policy of Richelieu and was on its way to becoming the next art center of Europe.

Indeed, Henriet made such a success of his venture with Callot that after the latter's death he acquired many other plates that belonged to the artist's own stock at Nancy. Henriet's nephew eventually inherited the print business, and after the nephew others in the family carried it on, thus forming a dynasty of print dealers, all of whom kept Callot's prints alive and available. This is how Jacques Callot's work found its permanent home in the French capital.

Plate 63. View of the Louvre. The longer building at right in this print is the Palace of the Louvre. The taller building to the right of the Louvre is the Petit Bourbon Palace, where Callot lodged with Henriet

Lorraine did not become a part of France until 150 years after Callot died, but by that time he already occupied a firm place in French art history. Callot of Lorraine had absorbed French culture through the old bond that existed between his land and France, and in his mirror of the world the French saw reflections of their own spirit: a love of fashions, elegant festivals and delicate fantasy, and of tales and anecdotes presented with grace and liveliness.

Callot, as if to repay the French in advance for their unending affection, gave them more than the official pictures of "The Siege of the Isle of Ré" and "The Siege of La Rochelle." In 1630, he etched of his own accord two enchanting views of the French capital: "View of the Pont Neuf" and "View of the Louvre" [PL. 63] each showing the oldest, best-loved, and eternal part of the city, the heart of Paris where the River Seine flows past memorable landmarks and everything is bathed with light. "View of the Pont Neuf" offers glimpses of everyday life on the Seine. "View of the Louvre" gives a royal water festival in full swing on the river; boats carry passengers from the silken world of the court, and from the masts stream long pennants sprinkled with the fleur-de-lis, symbol of French royalty. This was Callot's last rendering of a city festival.

Detail, plate 63

FOURTEEN

At Home in the Public Square

Callot's life had more than one layer. Peel back the Paris layer, and you find that during the period, from early 1629 to early 1631, when Callot was making his trips to the French capital to work for King Louis, he led an active life in his native Lorraine.

Lorraine, too, had become a part of history's mainstream. This was bound to happen to a little buffer state lying between France and the Hapsburgs. Young Duke Charles had not yet officially declared his political position, but he continued to flaunt his pro-Hapsburg sympathies, and twice before the end of 1631, he welcomed lengthy visits from Gaston of Orleans (whose reconciliation with brother Louis at the beginning of 1630 proved of short duration).

Callot's headquarters were at the small house he and his wife still kept in the row of houses on the public square in Nancy. He may be glimpsed there in a print by one of his pupils, which bears the caption: "The Room of Sieur Callot in the year 1630 and the manner in which he works. Francois Collignon, his pupil, drew and etched this."

✖ A SPECIAL VIEW OF CALLOT

Pupil Collignon was no great artist, but thanks are due him for providing an intriguing view. The room has a beam ceiling and resembles the orderly chamber of a private home. Callot, small as a gnome, is under a window at the far end of the room, sitting very upright as he draws energetically on a plate supported almost vertically by an easel resting on the table before him. Here and there are two flea-sized apprentices busy at unknown tasks. An article of furniture resembling a canopied and curtained bed stands against the wall to the viewer's right. It looks so huge that one wonders whether it could not be something built to hold Callot's plates and prints—impossible to say, because the curtains are drawn. The opposite wall contains high niches, each with a bust of a Roman emperor staring out upon the room. Below the emperors are a few strong, broad-bottom, straight-backed chairs of the period.

On such a chair, Gaston of Orleans, the rebellious, rakish young brother of King Louis, might comfortably have plunked his fattish self, for Gaston liked to come over from the palace and visit Callot. A time arrived when, according to biographer Felibien, "Gaston went every day with Count Maleuvrier to Callot's dwelling, where he spent two hours learning to draw."

Gaston's studies under Callot bore no fruit, but Callot himself made something permanent out of an acquaintance with the flighty prince. Forty-two "Landscapes" done in pen and ink by Callot to serve as drawing models for Gaston are vigorous and of lasting interest to art lovers.

There is, in addition, the handsome series of "Coins" that Callot etched for Gaston, who took a princely interest in coinage. The series consists of ten plates offering a total of 106 specimens. The items reflect Gaston's politics and are mostly coins then currently used in kingdoms, duchies, principalities, and other states ruled by or sympathetic toward the Hapsburgs. The obverse and the reverse of each coin are given side by side, with the obverse usually carrying the portrait of a Hapsburg or a pro-Hapsburg sovereign, and the reverse, the Hapsburg's double-headed eagle.

Some of the coins held personal associations for Callot

Detail. Coins.
The double-headed eagle
of the Hapsburg dynasty
appears on two of these
coins etched by Callot
late in his career. All
three coins are from a
series made for Gaston,
the French king's brother

and provided him with food for thought. One coin bore
the image of Regent Isabella of the Spanish Netherlands.
Since her victory at Breda, she had been suffering from poor
health and changing fortunes. Rumor had it that she was
now pawning her jewels to pay the soldiers sent by Spain
to fight the battles in the Netherlands. But the old Regent
remained staunchly loyal to the Spanish crown, and it was
no secret that she continued to support Gaston and Charles
in their conspiracies against King Louis and Richelieu.

Charles forever dreamed of fighting France. He continued to seek allies and enlarge his small army with mercenaries from abroad, and perhaps it was these mercenaries
who brought the plague with them in their infected clothes
or baggage. Anyway, the plague, that dreadful by-product
of the wars that were disrupting Europe, entered Lorraine
and Nancy. Though it preferred the poorer, ill-kept dis-
tricts of the city, it lay in wait for everyone and flared up,
declined, and flared up again. There were weeks when
church bells throughout the small country seemed never to
cease tolling for the dead.

✳ PLAGUE IN LORRAINE

In the latter half of 1630 the plague raged with special violence at Nancy. In August Callot's father died. Whether
Sieur Jean's death was due to the plague or some other cause
is not known. His last days, like most of his life, remain obscure, and of his end it can only be said that he died a poor
man, leaving an impoverished widow. One of his daughters
had married her Lorrainer. His eldest son, Jean II, was now
Herald of Arms and Superintendent of the Ducal Palace.
He had a large brood of children to support. Old Sieur
Jean's other children were priests or nuns, with the exception of Jacques, who happened to be in Paris.

Upon his father's death, Jacques was summoned home to
help settle family affairs. Then he went back to Paris and

wound up his work on the "Sieges" for King Louis. He returned home for good in early 1631. It was he, the prosperous artist, who purchased from the other heirs the family estate at Bainville-sur-Madon, in his beloved Lorraine countryside, about ten miles from Nancy.

Henceforth Jacques and his wife would have this easily accessible retreat of their own whenever the plague became an epidemic in the city. They might even go farther afield to their property at Houdemont, where Callot enjoyed hunting privileges. A charming miniature booklet, "The Prodigal Son" (etched in 1631) shows a lovely country chateau which is said to represent the one at Houdemont. In any case, the artist placed the Callot coat of arms above an entrance in the courtyard.

The persistence of the plague, which indeed never departed from Callot's Lorraine, left an impact on his production. These were the years when he etched many religious prints for his sickness-ridden compatriots. His "Martyrdom of St. Sebastian," a handsome plate featuring the saint who acted as intercessor against the plague, was a picture that could be hung on the walls of one's home. "Mysteries of the Life of Jesus" offered tiny pictures, any of which might be worn in a locket around one's neck as a protection against the scourge. He also embarked on a lengthy project, "Book of Saints for Every Day of the Year," which was to end up with 488 little pictures of saints, some showing scenes from their martyrdoms. "Book of Saints" had not been completed by the end of 1631, which closed a period in Callot's life. He had left his Paris days well behind him and cast his personal fortunes with the destiny of Lorraine.

Plate 64. St. John.
In one of his most graceful
religious etchings, Callot,
as a mature artist, depicted
St. John the Evangelist
exorcising an evil spirit

FIFTEEN

'Miseries' and 'Punishments'

In 1632 Callot etched a full-length portrait of Lorraine's Court Painter, Claude Deruet. Rivalry between the two artists had become a thing of the past, and Callot had even stood as godfather to Deruet's infant daughter. Friendship, however, did not keep the portrait from becoming the most revealing one that Callot ever made.

It is that of a courtier who has blustered his way to success. The haughty scowl fails to hide an emptiness behind the forehead. But Deruet would not notice his defects. He would admire the fine figure that he cuts with his dominating tread, papal decoration, elegantly tailored clothes and the handsome, gay young son beside him. Lastly, sprawling in the background is the huge mansion that Deruet has built for his residence near the gates of Nancy—an edifice so impressive that it had been nicknamed "The Louvre." The print tells the world that Claude Deruet is a man of consequence.

In the eyes of the world, Callot himself has not done badly. He owns country estates and the little town house where royalty drops in; he has proper clothes for country, town, or court. An inventory (made in 1635, but representing the kind of finery at his disposal in the better year of 1632) lifts a curtain on a well-stocked wardrobe which includes a suit of red damask, two black taffeta cloaks, a hooded, sleeved cloak of grey-black Berry cloth, and a cloak of dried-rose Spanish cloth, plush-lined and trimmed with gold and silver lace. Such was the peacock-like attire he wore as he walked the cobblestones of Nancy, planning some new picture, or mulling over the crisis caused in Lorraine by the imprudent Duke Charles and the flippant Gaston of Orleans.

✠ A SECRET MARRIAGE AND POLITICAL TROUBLE

On January 3, 1632, Gaston married Charles's sister, Marguerite of Lorraine. Charles, who was abroad on Hapsburg affairs, had consented to the union. The ceremony took place secretly, behind the closed doors of a Nancy convent, but Gaston, in a prankish mood, had previously let it be noised about that he was madly in love with Marguerite. The rumors of a romance involving the Heir Presumptive to the throne of France had alarmed the King and Cardinal Richelieu.

To prevent such a marriage, and at the same time to keep down pro-Hapsburg Charles, France had sent an army to Metz, a bishopric long held by the French within Lorraine. Louis and Richelieu came too, and Charles was brought home promptly by his father to appear before the King. The meeting took place at the Lorraine town of Vic. There, on January 6, three days after Gaston's marriage, Charles signed a treaty by which he handed over to France the town of Marsal (Callot's wife had lived there). Charles also agreed to behave in a more friendly manner toward France, and he gave his word that he would never permit his sister to marry Gaston. Of course, the promise about Gaston and Marguerite was utterly false—a little matter which Richelieu, who soon learned the truth, would not forget.

Meanwhile, the display of French power at Vic had frightened Gaston. He showed his colors by abandoning his bride and fleeing to his mother, the exiled Marie de'

Medici, at Brussels. There, with Regent Isabella's help, he raised a few troops, and in the spring he accompanied them through eastern Lorraine on his way to join an anti-Richelieu faction in southern France. He fought down there for a while and then made peace with King Louis. The military support that Charles had hoped to secure from Gaston never materialized. All Charles ever got out of the friendship was the troublesome union of his sister, who stayed on at Nancy.

Charles continued his anti-French activities, and sober Lorrainers wondered if their young Duke was not rash in antagonizing Richelieu at the wrong time. Charles could not wage war against France without the help of allies, and although some of these, like Regent Isabella and Maximilian of Bavaria, were more substantial than Gaston, they could not lend immediate aid because they had battles of their own to fight.

THE INDEPENDENCE OF LORRAINE IS THREATENED BY FRANCE

Richelieu on his side found the time ripe for attempting to gain control of Lorraine. He had recently entered the ever-spreading Thirty Years' War by allying himself with a new, heroic arrival on the battlefields: Sweden's Gustavus Adolphus, the Golden King who sailed down from the North to uphold the Protestant cause.

These wars may seem to have made strange companions in arms, but actually, the old quarrel between Protestants and Catholics, though it mattered in the beginning, no longer concerned most leaders, least of all Cardinal Richelieu. To him, the Protestant Swedish King was a brilliant soldier and a powerful associate. Thus in June, 1632, six months after the Treaty of Vic, Richelieu induced King Louis to make a formal declaration of war against Lorraine and to send troops for a second time into the duchy.

Charles, who was proving himself less courageous in diplomacy than on the battlefield, lost no time in signing a new peace treaty at Liverdun. By this he ceded to France his towns of Clermont-en-Argonne, Dun, Stenay, and Jametz.

During the rest of 1632, Charles traveled beyond the borders of his duchy, mingling with Hapsburgs and lending them his troops. It was the year when his brother-in-law, Prince de Phalsbourg, whom Callot had etched once as a dashing general on horseback and again as Hercules atop a glittering chariot in the "Combat at the Barrier," fell in a battle in the Rhineland. Also, 1632 was the year when France's glorious ally, the Golden King of Sweden, was killed. He was riding his horse in the midst of a November battle at Lutzen (near Leipzig, Germany) when a bullet struck his head. His soldiers mourned him, and with vengeance at heart they followed the tide of war, under new leadership, westward toward Lorraine.

NANCY SEEMS SECURE FROM WAR

Nancy, situated near the middle of the 12,000-square-mile duchy, seemed secure enough from the onslaught of war. Old Charles III, the duke of Callot's boyhood, had seen to it that both the Old Town and the New Town of the capital were surrounded by a great zigzagging rampart that remained about as strong as any in Europe.

In the small house on the public square, Callot applied himself to his usual wide variety of plates. His output for 1632 includes, beside his portrait of Deruet, a series called "Large Apostles," rendered in vigorous, sculptural style and published within the year by Henriet of Paris; a palm-sized booklet, "Military Exercises," consisting of 13 plates of tiny warriors practicing airily with the weapons of the hour —swords, pikes, arquebuses, and cannon [PL. 65]—and published at a later date by Henriet; and a small plate, "Clashes of Cavalry," showing a lively military fracas

142

Plate 65. Cannon Firing. Two men practice firing a cannon in this small plate etched by Callot for his "Military Exercises"

Plate 66. A Battle. A violent cavalry battle, created by Callot, illustrates the horrors of war and the epic bravery of soldiers

Israel excud. cum P

etched in a kind of glory-be-to-battle manner. Callot also tried to etch some little scenes of a soldier's life. The smallness of these plates known as his "Small Miseries of War," cramped him, and he abandoned the series. Yet, he clung to the idea of portraying what the wars were really like beyond the walls of Nancy.

Early in the new year of 1633, young Duke Charles IV openly declared himself in favor of the Hapsburg Emperor, Ferdinand II. This made Lorraine officially at odds with France, whose troops were already stationed in the duchy. Charles nevertheless rode off to gather military laurels on foreign soil. He left a governor in charge of Nancy but did not bother to provide him with enough troops and supplies to repulse an enemy or endure a lengthy siege. The walls of Nancy seemed to Charles sufficient in themselves.

Within the walls life continued. There were the plague-stricken, of course, and many war refugees with tales of horror, yet a bright carnival took place in February, 1633. On March 31st Charles, wherever he was, found time to

sign a deed giving Callot a little plot of land near the public square. The reasons for the gift are lost to us, but the deed remains along with a contract that Callot signed on April 5th with a builder for the construction of a stable and coach-house on the plot. In the coach-house the artist was eventually to keep a four-wheeled, upholstered carriage that displayed a lining and roof made of embroidered blue serge.

On August 10th, at Pfaffenhoven in Alsace (the land bordering the eastern frontier of Lorraine) Charles's army met the Swedes and suffered a bloody defeat. Then the Swedes invaded Lorraine and began the destruction of the countryside.

A few days before the Battle of Pfaffenhoven the French Parliament, taking advantage of a feudal technicality, claimed possession of the important Lorraine district of Bar. Upon learning this, Duke Charles sent his young brother, Cardinal Nicholas Francis, to the French court to appease Richelieu. Cardinal Nicholas Francis, though he was the studious one who had attended the University at Pont-à-Mousson, could not match wits with Richelieu. The elder Cardinal demanded that Charles surrender his capital and his sister, the Duchess of Orleans Marguerite of Lorraine, who was still within its walls. Charles, upon hearing Richelieu's terms, refused to surrender his capital. He refused to hand over his sister to France. Her marriage to Gaston had been declared void by the French court, but she considered herself legitimately wed and awaited the day when she might join her husband at the Brussels court.

Cardinal Nicholas Francis went back to Richelieu, came home with the same terms as before, and Charles again refused them. However, Nicholas Francis did at least succeed in helping Marguerite escape. He had her dress herself as a page, and in this disguise she slipped through a gate in the walls of Nancy and through the French troops that were beginning to surround the capital. She headed for Brussels and arrived safely at her destination.

Detail, plate 66

144

❋ NANCY IS BESIEGED

As for the French troops, they had occupied Bar on August 25th, and on the 28th King Louis himself appeared at Pont-à-Mousson. On the 29th the French army laid siege to Nancy. Duke Charles should have been on hand to defend his capital, but there was just his governor, who lacked not only soldiers and supplies but definite instructions from the master of the realm. Charles's brave sister Henriette, widow of the Prince of Phalsbourg, moved through the city trying to arouse a fighting spirit in its defenders, but she did so in vain. The famous walls saw hardly a skirmish.

Charles, hoping that allies would soon come to his assistance, decided to mark time by sending Nicholas Francis to negotiate once more with Richelieu. A treaty which Nicholas Francis proceeded to sign on September 6th gave Nancy to the French for a period of four years. But the governor of Nancy, having received no orders from Charles, refused to open the city's gates to the enemy.

Finally, Charles, whom French troops had driven out of his town of Epinal, was invited to a conference with Richelieu. They met at Charmes, some 20 miles from Nancy, and there on September 20th the Duke signed a treaty not unlike the one negotiated by his brother. Afterward the Duke foolishly let Richelieu take him to King Louis's headquarters at Laneuville-before-Nancy. Charles received full honors from the King, but found himself a prisoner, and on September 21st he had to sign an order commanding his Nancy governor to open the gates of the capital.

It was September 25, 1633, when King Louis XIII made his solemn entrance into fallen Nancy. The crowds shouted, "Long live the King!" but he could sense their love for the defeated Duke and waived the offer to take up residence at the ducal palace. He stayed in painter Deruet's mansion and held court at Nancy for about a week.

Felibien describes an incident involving Callot which occurred soon after the King's entrance:

> The King, having reduced the town of Nancy to his obedience, sent for Callot and proposed that he depict this new conquest, as he had done with the capture of La Rochelle. But Callot most respectfully begged His Majesty to excuse him from this because he was a Lorrainer and believed he should do nothing against the honor of his Prince and against his country. The King accepted his plea, saying that the Duke of Lorraine was indeed fortunate in having such faithful and loving subjects. Several courtiers, objecting to Callot's refusal, told the King quite audibly that the artist should be forced to submit to His Majesty's wishes. Callot, having overheard this, replied quickly, with considerable courage, that he would cut off his thumb rather than do anything against his honor, if there were an attempt to compel him.

Detail, plate 66

"THE LARGE MISERIES OF WAR"

Callot did not etch the siege of Nancy. But during the year when Nancy fell, he etched some of his loveliest devotional pictures for a small 14-plate "Life of the Holy Virgin," and he presented lords and ladies in a 14-page miniature booklet called "Fantasies."

During that year he also reported on the war in another series of etchings. This series was published by Henriet in Paris as a book before the year ended. The title page reads, "The/ Miseries and the/ Disasters/ Of War/ Portrayed by Jacques Callot/ Lorraine Nobleman/ And brought to light by Israel/ his friend/ At Paris/ 1633/ With Privilege of the King." ("Brought to light" means "published"; "Israel" refers to the publisher, Israel Henriet, and "With Privilege of the King" signifies that a copyright was granted to the book.) The 18 plates in the series, each about 3 inches high and 7¼ inches wide, became popularly known as "The Large Miseries of War." Their size distinguishes them from the smaller series which Callot never completed.

The title page is ornamented with elegant, doll-faced officers ready to play the game of war. The print, "Enlistment

of Troops," is a tidy scene in which men sign up against a background of orderly platoons. "A Battle," showing the drama of a cavalry encounter filled with smoke, fallen riders, and dead horses, corresponds with what Callot's public might expect in a war print [PL. 66]. In the final scene a young prince sits on his throne while his soldiers receive awards for bravery. It is the intervening scenes, however, that struck a new note by revealing the unheroic miseries which befell both soldier and civilian behind the actual line of battle.

The history of Europe abounded with wars, and artists had not always been spared the experience of them. Yet, in Callot's time, the miseries of a contemporary war had rarely been portrayed by artists except in terms of allegory or hidden meanings. Art had usually stressed the glory of battle and the joy of conquest. Artists either had not dared to provoke the displeasure of the lords or had not found it interesting or profitable to depict a war-torn landscape. Callot, in his victory picture, "Siege of Breda," had provided a few incidental glimpses of war's attendant horrors. In his "Large Miseries" he brought the horrors sharply into focus. For nearly 200 years, until the Spanish artist Goya picked up the theme and etched a series known as "The Disasters of War," Callot's "Large Miseries" were to remain the unrivaled report on what can happen to human beings when the barriers of peace are broken.

When Callot etched his "Large Miseries," The Thirty Years' War was midway in its course but had not changed in character since its beginning, when the gentle Winter King, after accompanying his troops in a retreat through neutral territory, complained: "There should be some difference between friend and foe. But these [soldiers] destroy both. . . . I believe these men are possessed of the devil; they delight in setting fire to everything."

One reason for this ravaging was that the common soldiers were usually mercenaries, brutal by nature, and fighting for no cause. Then, too, they did not always receive pay; often their only recompense came from their plunder. Pay or no pay, plunder was the rule of the day. Tough General Mansfeld, whose army had crossed Lorraine in 1622 in search of food, said: "When the gate of plunder is open to the soldiers, they enter larger areas of liberty. . . . They spare no one, no matter what his quality may be, and respect no place however holy, neither Churches, Altars, Tombs, Sepulchres nor the dead bodies that lie therein." But Mansfeld realized, as did the other leaders, that an effective means of winning a war was to ruin the enemy's land. Of course, many outrages occurred simply from the custom of quartering soldiers with the civilian population. Duke Charles's own mercenaries had wrought havoc among the country people of Lorraine; so had the French army of occupation and other invading troops. Callot must have seen some horrors with his own eyes while he traveled through the Lorraine countryside. The rest he gathered by listening.

✺ WAR AS CALLOT SHOWS IT

In his "Large Miseries," soldier and civilian, friend and foe share the misfortunes of war. Callot shows soldiers who plunder and burn a convent and abduct the nuns. There are soldiers raiding a tavern [PL. 67]. Elsewhere, peasants with scythes and flails attack the soldiers. Robbers, who might be soldiers or civilians, loot a stagecoach, since lawlessness has become contagious. Often, crime is the only way to get money to buy bread.

Soldiers are frequently punished for their crimes. Callot's "Hangman's Tree" [PL. 68] is a military camp scene, showing swarms of condemned men dangling like pods from branches of the tree. In other scenes, by other methods, including the firing squad and the wheel, military authorities mete out death penalties to soldiers for their crimes, of which desertion is surely one.

Plate 67. **Plundering a Tavern. Soldiers run off** with the pots, pans, and clothes of poor civilians in one of Callot's etchings from his series called "The Large Miseries of War"

Plate 68. The Hangman's Tree. One of Callot's best known works, this print depicts the wholesale manner in which men were punished for wartime crimes during The Thirty Years' War

The soldier's life in wartime is not easy, nor is the life of a civilian in a war zone any easier. Disaster strikes indiscriminately. Witness the scene [PL. 69] where crippled men in uniform and starving beggars in civilian rags line up outside a hospital; or that dusty landscape where men—

they could be soldiers or civilians—lie dying by the road-side. Such was The Thirty Years' War.

Callot followed the war series with a single plate known as "The Punishments" [PL. 70]. In five plates of his "Large Miseries" he had shown corporal punishment inflicted on men for crimes in war time. But corporal punishment also thrived in days of peace and had been a familiar sight to him since he was a boy. His Lorraine, the Lorraine of the Counter Reformation, believed commonly that men were born evil and that their wickedness could only be overcome through divine law by means of punishment. A death sentence was often carried out with horrible torture, such as quartering a man's body by horses. At Nancy, the executions were held outdoors in public, the theory being that the sight of suffering would deter spectators from committing crimes of their own. Actually, the populace delighted in watching executions.

In his "Punishments" (1634) Callot depicts ten prevailing forms of corporal punishment, including burning at the stake, all in action on the one small plate. The setting is the sunny square of an unidentified city, crowded with enthralled spectators. The picture at a first glance seems a festival of punishments. But Callot, although he paid careful attention to technical details, reduced everything to a tiny scale that permits no emphasis on brutality for brutality's sake. He has stationed priests here and there, holding up crosses in absolution of the dying. His "Punishments" is a documentary on the penal code.

Plate 69. The Hospital. Another scene from the "Large Miseries" shows wounded, maimed, and homeless men seeking help

Plate 70. Punishments. In this single etching, Callot grouped the common methods of his day for physically punishing civilians who were judged guilty of crimes

Detail, plate 70

Israel ex. cum privil. Regis.

Supplicium Sceleri Fraenum

The Final Scene

Jacques Callot had almost completed his record of the world. His time was running out. Felibien reports of Callot that "Although he was moderate in his habits and manner of life, he did not enjoy very robust health. He was inconvenienced by a stomach ailment brought about by his ordinary work and by the fatigue which he had long endured because of engraving always in a stooped position. Thus, a few years before his death, whenever he engraved he held himself upright before an easel, as painters work."

Felibien goes on to say that "Whether the infirmity that Callot had suffered from his youth because of a bent stomach or whether something else produced a growth of flesh in his stomach, this irregularity increased. . . ." In the light of present medical knowledge Callot's ailment is believed to have been a form of stomach ulcer. Whatever it was, he experienced great bodily discomfort along with mental anguish as he watched the fortunes of his country go from bad to worse.

Duke Charles of Lorraine, who in September, 1633 had surrendered his capital for a period of four years, found it hard to rule under the hostile occupation of the French. On January 19, 1634, he passed the crown to his young brother, Cardinal Nicholas Francis, and departed from the land to fight for the Hapsburgs.

Within a few weeks, good Nicholas Francis also departed. He had realized what the French were planning. The French considered that the lawful sovereign of Lorraine was Charles's wife, Nicole, and that since she was childless the duchy, upon her death, would pass to her sister Claude. They would marry Claude to a French prince so that the duchy could be attached as a province of France. Nicholas Francis nipped those plans in the bud. He had not yet taken Holy Orders, and on February 18th, while staying at Luneville, he absolved himself from his bonds with the Church, and immediately he married Claude. The French soon learned of this, escorted him and his bride to Nancy and kept them virtual prisoners at the ducal palace. On April 1st, Nicholas Francis and Claude escaped in disguise and began their successful journey toward a permanent home at Vienna.

The stage was set for Charles's return to Lorraine. He had been a foolish duke; he had heaped disasters upon Lorraine; he had abdicated and departed from the realm. But to the ancient nobility and to his officers and many other loyal Lorrainers, he was still the Duke, and they awaited the day when he would regain his throne. They believed the Hapsburgs were bound to help him in exchange for the service he was rendering them on foreign battlefields. He distinguished himself with notable valor on the bloody field of Nordlingen in September, 1634, where the Hapsburg Catholic armies crushed those of the Protestant Germans and the Swedes. But Regent Isabella of the Spanish Netherlands had died, and aid from other Hapsburg sources was not forthcoming. Charles did not return in 1634.

During that year France seized Charles's fortresses one by one, even though they were often stoutly defended to the bitter end.

※ AN OATH IS DEMANDED

At Nancy, in October, the French governor demanded that the notables in the capital sign an oath of allegiance to King Louis. Not until December, near the deadline for complying with this law, did Jacques Callot appear before the

authorities to write his name in the register. He came with
a few gentlemen, including his brother Jean, who was still
Herald of Arms.

During 1634, in spite of the misfortunes of Lorraine and
in spite of his bad health, Jacques Callot continued to produce pictures at his home on the public square of Nancy.
No doubt he followed as best he could the routine that
Felibien attributed to him:

> He regulated his time so well that after rising quite early in
> the morning he went immediately with his elder brother to
> walk outside the City. Next, after hearing Mass, he worked
> until dinner time. Right after midday he paid a few calls, so as
> not to return too quickly to work, and then he resumed his
> labor until evening, having with him almost invariably a few
> friends who watched him working and conversed with him.

It was the year when, in addition to "Punishments," he
etched his greatest flight of fantasy, "The Temptation of
St. Anthony" [PL. 71]. This was a second interpretation
of a theme that he had tried as a young man in Florence.
The early version had been playful and loosely composed.
In the new one he corrected those faults and proved himself a true heir to the fantasy of Bosch and Breughel.

At first sight his composition gives an impression of
sprightly music; but upon inspection the winged demons,
the fire-spitting dragons, and other monsters that beset St.
Anthony become terrifying, none more so than the one
shaped like a cannon and belching daggers, pikes, and other
weapons of The Thirty Years' War.

The new year, 1635, ushered in Lorraine's worst period
of agony. Hope persisted that Duke Charles would return;
if he did, he would find a land in ruins. Plague and famine
stalked the duchy, and refugees who flocked to Nancy said
that elsewhere the people lived on grass, carrion, and human flesh. They said that Richelieu, in anger against Duke
Charles, was stationing Swedish troops in the countryside
and that the Swedes carried banners on which there was a
human figure split from head to foot, surrounded by sol-

Detail, plate 71

diers holding in one hand a sword and in the other a lighted torch, and beneath it all there was the word "Lorraine." The fact was that soldiers and marauders of almost every nationality were looting and ruining the helpless duchy.

CALLOT PREPARES HIS WILL

Felibien tells us that the conditions in Lorraine made Callot resolve to go with his wife to Florence: "there to live and work in peace for the rest of his days." Callot's health, however, intervened. Yet his etchings give no indication that the hand that held the needle was not as sure as ever. In early 1635, a major project, a series of scenes from the New Testament, was undertaken in Callot's most delicate manner. But on March 5th, he began to make his will:

> In the name of the Father and of the Son and of the Holy Ghost, Amen. I, Jacques Callot, Engraver to His Highness [the Duke of Lorraine], and dwelling at Nancy, being of sound mind and judgment (though afflicted with illness) have made and devised my testament in accordance with my last will in the form and manner that follows, to wit, that as it has pleased God to redeem me by the merits of his precious blood, Our Saviour and Redeemer Jesus Christ, I resign myself into the arms of His Divine Providence, wishing to die as I have lived in the Catholic, Apostolic and Roman Faith and Religion, beseeching, when it pleases Him to call me from this world into the other, the assistance of the glorious Virgin Mary, of all the blessed Saints in Paradise and particularly of Saint Jacques, my patron. . . .

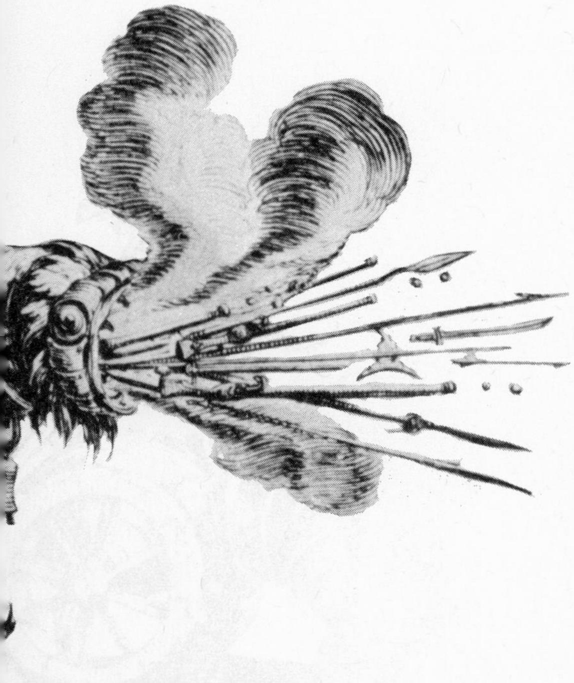

The will goes on to express Callot's wish that he be buried at Nancy alongside his forefathers in the Church of the Franciscans, and that an epitaph be placed on his tomb. Provision is made for a Mass to be said there for his soul. A Mass shall be said in several other churches that he designates, and a Mass shall be said in the Church of the Franciscans each year on the anniversary of his death. One of those other churches is to receive money to buy an altar table in the name of St. Francis of Paul to whom Callot, in

Plate 71. Temptation of St. Anthony (second version) In Callot's second etching on this subject, some of his devils carry pitchforks as they did in his first work (see pl. 16). However, the strong influence of The Thirty Years' War on the artist's mind and work can be easily seen. One cannonlike monster fires daggers, pikes, and halberds, while a demon at lower right brandishes his own musket. This scene of torture and destruction is, perhaps, Callot's greatest flight of fantasy

the words of the will, "has always felt a special devotion." The body of the will comes next but makes no mention of the copper plates that have brought him wordly success. Being childless, he leaves most of his real estate and furnishings to his wife, although his brother Jean is left a share and also receives a gift of money. Callot's widowed, impoverished mother receives a yearly income for the rest of her days. "My wife and I have often spoken of this," he says. A small sum of money goes to a younger sister Jeanne, who is a Franciscan nun. To the husband of the youngest sister goes a stallion.

On March 18th, three days after making his will, Callot adds wording in which he bequeaths a small sum of money to a younger brother George, who is a Franciscan friar. Other small sums are set aside for his man servant, a maid, and for the nurse who is taking care of him. He then makes known his decision about the copper plates that he engraved. Half of those found in his possession at the time of his death go to his wife, the other half to his elder brother Jean in recognition of "the honor, respect and kind services which Jean Callot, my dear brother, has shown and rendered me, and the little benefit I have allotted him in my aforesaid will, and in consideration of the gifts which it has pleased God to grant me, and because of the great burden of children whom my brother must support."

Callot had about 300 plates in his possession; the rest were scattered far and wide. Some had remained with the sovereigns, friars, booksellers, and private patrons who commissioned them; others he had given or sold to friends. Quite a few had gone to his Paris publisher, Henriet. In future years scholars were to be kept busy tracking down all the plates. Today, in the great Lieure picture-catalog of Callot's work, the number of his illustrations stands at 1,428, an impressive total made possible through the speedy etching technique he had developed and his unending application to his art.

On March 24, 1635, six days after bequeathing his plates,

Jacques Callot died at Nancy. His age was 43, his talent at full tide. The bells of old Nancy tolled for him, and he was buried according to his wishes in the cloisters of the Church of the Franciscans, which was the final resting place of the Dukes of Lorraine.

❈ AN EPITAPH
FOR THE MASTER

At Paris his young friend and fellow artist, Abraham Bosse, etched a plate commemorating Callot. The print shows a simple, shaftlike monument surmounted by a sculptured bust. Callot has a serene and kindly oval face, a broad and thoughtful forehead. Down the side of the monument run the words of an epitaph, written as though he himself were speaking. They begin:

> To Posterity
>
> Passer-by, cast your eyes upon this writing, and you shall know how far my journey has been advanced; you will not be grieved if I slightly delay your own. I am Jacques Callot, that great and excellent engraver who reposes at this spot, awaiting the resurrection of bodies. My birth was indifferent, my rank noble, my life short and happy; but my renown has been and will be without parallel. No one has been my equal in all manner of accomplishments pertaining to drawing and engraving on copper. All the earth has consented to the extraordinary praises that have been given me, without my ever, on that account, having departed from my natural modesty. I was born at Nancy in the year 1594 [1592], and I died likewise at Nancy on March 25 [24], 1635: to the incredible regret of Lorraine, my native land, and of all the rare spirits of our century, and principally of Catherine Kuttinger, my wife. . . .

The rest of the epitaph is conventional. Those opening lines are the ones that are memorable. Bosse made a couple of errors in dates, but his summing-up of Callot has a validity based on firsthand knowledge.

Henriet, the publisher, had also known Callot very well. Their friendship had stretched through a lifetime. Henriet realized how much Callot's art had meant to people, rich

Detail, plate 71

and poor, far and wide. Callot had provided them with religious images that brought comfort; he had delighted them with fantasies and, above all, he had given them visual representations of what was happening in the world. He had been Europe's first great reporter-artist. To Henriet's way of thinking, Callot himself should tell the public of his own departure.

Among Callot's possessions at Nancy, Henriet found a small plate, known as "The Little Trellis" [PL. 72]. He inscribed along the bottom of it: "The last plate of the late Callot, to which the acid was not applied until after his death." Then Henriet issued prints from this plate, and they began their long, unending travels through Europe and beyond.

"The Little Trellis" deals not with blessed saints in Paradise, nor with fantasies of the imagination, nor with mis-

Plate 72. The Little Trellis. The artist's last work is a scene of peace and happiness, showing ladies and gentlemen dining at a country inn. According to the inscription, the plate (shown here in its original size) was not printed until after Callot's death

eries on earth, but with the good life that the world can offer. The scene shows a party of gentlemen and their ladies dining outdoors beneath the trellis of a country inn. Here, while the inhabitants of the inn contentedly pursue their daily tasks, one gentleman in the party plays a lute, his lady strums a harp, and their companions raise goblets to toast the brightness of the moment, a moment made everlasting by Jacques Callot.

Detail, plate 72

Bibliography

BALDINUCCI, F., *Notizie de' professori del disegno da Cimabue in qua*, Florence, 1681. Second edition, Florence, G. B. Stecchi, 1767-1774, in 21 vols. (Callot, vol. XIV, 1772, pp. 128-153).

BECHTEL, EDWIN DE T., *Jacques Callot*, New York, Braziller, 1955.

BOSSE, ABRAHAM, *Traicté des manières de graver en taille douce . . .*, Paris, Bosse, 1645.

BOSSE, ABRAHAM, *Sentimens sur la distinction des diverses manières de peinture, dessein et graveure*, Paris, Chez l'auteur, 1649.

BRUWAERT, EDMOND, *Vie de Jacques Callot, graveur lorrain 1592-1635*, Paris, Imprimerie Nationale, 1912, "Société pour l'étude de la gravure française").

BRUWAERT, EDMOND, *Jacques Callot et don Giovanni de' Medici*, Paris, Gazette des Beaux-Arts, 1924. (periode 5, tome 9, pp. 118-127).

FÉLIBIEN, ANDRÉ, *Entretiens sur les vies et sur les ouvrages des plus excellens peintres anciens et modernes . . . ;* quatrième partie, Paris, S. Mabre-Cramoisy, 1685.

LIEURE, J., *Jacques Callot*. 5 vols., I-II, première partie: *La vie artistique;* III-V, deuxième partie: *Catalogue de l'oeuvre gravé.* Introduction by F. Courboin. Paris, Gazette des Beaux-Arts, 1924-1927.

MAROT, PIERRE, *Jacques Callot d'après des documents inédits*, Nancy-Paris-Strasbourg, Berger-Levrault, 1939.

MEAUME, ÉDOUARD, *Recherches sur la vie et les ouvrages de Jacques Callot*, Nancy, 1853; Paris, Vᵛᵉ Jules Renouard, 1860, 2 vols.

TERNOIS, DANIEL, *L'Art de Jacques Callot*, Paris, De Nobele, 1962.

TERNOIS, DANIEL, *Jacques Callot, Catalogue complet de son oeuvre dessiné*, Paris, De Nobele, 1962.

The following books about the period in which Jacques Callot lived or about his work are recommended for further reading:

The Three Musketeers, Alexandre Dumas' swashbuckling novel, graphically portrays some of the France Callot knew. C. V. Wedgwood's *The Thirty Years War*, available in a paperback edition (Doubleday Anchor Books, 1961), gives an excellent account of war as it was conducted in Callot's day. Edwin De T. Bechtel's *Jacques Callot* (Braziller, 1955) is more accessible than other sources listed in the Bibliography, and it presents in concise and scholarly form many fine reproductions of Callot prints.

Index